MICHELE S A E E :

Buildings + Projects

MICHELE S A E E :

Buildings + Projects

Introduction by
Thom Mayne
Essays by
Aris Janigian,
Frédéric Migayrou,
and Michele Saee

RIZZOLI
NEW YORK

First published in the United States of
America in 1997 by
RIZZOLI INTERNATIONAL PUBLICATIONS, INC.
300 Park Avenue South, New York,
NY 10010

Copyright © 1997 by
Rizzoli International Publications, Inc.
Introduction © Thom Mayne
"Michele Saee: Imminent Architecture"
© Frédéric Migayrou
"Forget It: What the Body Does Best When
Left to Itself" © Aris Janigian

Library of Congress Cataloging-in-Publication Data

Saee, Michele
    Michele Saee : buildings + projects / introduction by Thom Mayne:
    essays by Aris Janigian, Frédéric Migayrou, and Michele Saee.
        p. cm.
    Includes bibliographical references.
    ISBN 0-8478-1994-9 (pb)
    1. Saee, Michele—Themes, motives. 2. Building (Architectural
    firm) 3. Architecture, Postmodern—California, Southern.
    I. Migayrou, Frédéric. II. Title.
    NA737.S315S24 1997   97-11861
    720'.92—dc21   CIP

Designed by April Greiman, Los Angeles

Front cover illustration:
Front facade, Ecru Marina Clothing Store,
Marina del Rey, 1990.
Photograph by Marvin Rand;
Digital image by April Greiman.

Printed and bound in Singapore

Photo Credits
Numbers refer to page numbers:

Roland Bishop
18-20, 22, 26

Benny Chan
28, 29, 32 center right, 33, 35-37

Peter Cook
58, 59, 61 top right, 64-65, 67-69, 71 top
& bottom right, 90-93, 100 bottom left, 102-103

Gabor Ekecs
120-123

April Greiman (digital imagery)
25, 32, 49, 53, 56, 64-65 background, 68, 79,
82-83, 93, 110 center top, 112, 114, 116
backgrounds

Tim Street-Porter
19-22, 24, 25 top left

Stefani Weisler
34-35, 72-73, 76-77

Scott Wright
25 top left

Marvin Rand
50-52, 54, 56 top right, 57, 80 center left,
81, 84, 96, 98, 100 top & center left, 101,
105, 107, 110 center & bottom left, 112, 113-
117, 118 center, 119 center bottom, 125, 133
top center, 134, 136, 137-139, 142-143, 148-
149, 150-151, 153, 155

Contents

I tell you that I have long way to go before I am where one begins.

You are so young, so before all beginnings, and I want to beg you, as much as I can, to be patient toward all that is unsolved in your heart and to try to love the questions themselves like locked rooms and like books that are written in a very foreign tongue.

Do not now seek the answers, which cannot be given you because you would not be able to live them.
And the point is, to live everything.

Live the question now. Perhaps you will then gradually, without noticing it, live along some distant day into the answer.

Resolve to be always beginning to be a beginner!

"Love and other difficulties"
R.M. Rilke

I dedicate this book

to my parents

Sharifeh and Nasser.

Special thanks to my wife Arezou, our daughter
Sayeh, and our son Alisina

Acknowledgments

Architecture is by
its nature the work
of many people. As
I look back at the
past decade I see
this work as the
culmination of
many voices and
unique talents
graciously contrib-
uting to a common
vision. It has been
an honor to have
received the gifts
of their talents, the
energy of their
processes, and the
influence of their
wisdom. Among
those individuals
whom I would
especially like to
thank are:

Joe Abrajano
Aaron Betsky
Florence Blecher
Jillian Burt
Marie Christopher
Geoff Colin
Jonathan Day
Marty Doscher
Mike Fink
Michael Fouther
Nick Gillock
Ron Golan
Nardin Golparvaran
Richard Heinz
Lousine Hogtanian
Terry Hudak
Farhad Kharestan
Elmar Kleiner
Melissa La'O
Thomas Leerberg
David Lindberg
Jason Luke
Richard Lundquist
Eric Marable
Max Massie
Marni Nelco
Kaoru Orime
Kelly Owens
Chloe Parent
Clive Piercy
Elizabeth Plessen
Sandep Rahi
Bryan Richard
Eric Rosen
Joan Simon
John Scott
Sam Solhaug
Emiko Teragawa
Miguel de la Torre
Shiraz
Hernan M. Munayco
Yassaman Vafai
Azin Valy
Myung Yang

I am grateful for the
guidance and the
advice I have received
in the process of
creating this mono-
graph. I would espe-
cially like to thank:

Malcolm Ball
Mehzad Beglari
Miguel Castillo
J.C. Chung
Roy Dehbibi
Michael Gallucci
Saul Goldin
Marty Herling
Dave Jeffers
Danny Diaz
Barna Stubner
John McCoy
Vince Naso
Andrew Nasser
Pierre Riopel
John Rotondi
Tony Singaus
Charles So
Roland Tso

To those who contributed to
this monograph, thanks for
your dedication and your
vision:

Julie Eakins
April Greiman
Aris Janigian
Thom Mayne
Megan McFarland
Frédéric Migayrou
David Morton
Bryan Richard
Louise L. Rosa
Julie Taylor
Lorna Turner

And to Marvin Rand-
for your wisdom and your
belief in this work.

Introduction
by Thom Mayne

The assertion of individual experience and its inherent therapeutic possibilities, coupled with the search for a transformative method, are the themes that Michele Saee reiterates in his texts and which are apparent in his work. His passion is to find his own affinities among unlikely influences, to make architecture that is receptive to found forces. He defines this architecture as "a container of consciousness," and he arrives at it through a strategy of living with awareness. Sensation, memory, imagination, and unlearning or unseeing the ordinary symbols of experience all play a role in Saee's process and reveal his aspiration to an architecture as enigmatic and dense as being itself.

Like e.e. cummings, Saee regards dullness and neutrality as his deepest enemies. Art critic Donald Kuspit discusses the artist's special authority, integrity, and power as qualities fundamental to the avant-garde: the artist is able to be him or herself in a way that is impossible for other people and experiences without mediation what is fundamental or original in the spontaneous experience, so that experience remains unmitigated by convention. Why is spontaneous expression so important to Saee's aesthetic? Because while all of us have both intellectual and emotional potential, these are realized only to the extent that they are spontaneously expressed. Erich Fromm identified this notion as positive freedom (freedom to versus freedom from), which consists of the spontaneous activity of the "total integrated personality." Immanuel Kant assigned the aesthetic a special position between sensuousness and reason, which is where I think the adventurousness of Saee's architectural inventions is found. His is an architecture that challenges the isolation of mind from feeling.

Saee's optimism should not be confused with the early modernists' heroic adaptation of Nietzsche's salvation of art, suggested in his assertion that, as Kuspit notes, what is essential in art is its perfection of existence, its essential affirmation and deification of existence. Saee's instinct for architecture's therapeutic value operates at a more personal level; his ambitions are directed toward the individual as opposed to society. Working in the United States, which among industrially developed countries is unusual in terms of its rigid ideological control system, his stance is closer to that of resistance—a resistance that aspires to transform reality and detach it from the service of external power. His hope represents an optimism that, I think, is manifested in work rooted in the provisional idea of emergence; and in Saee's devotion to a philosophy of becoming and rebirth there is a strong Bergsonian twist. His questions come from comprehending and enjoying the world around him and from an instinctual awareness of emergence. Every project proceeds on a different, indeterminate course, actively engaged with the world interpreted as a potentiality.

To be modern is an act of historical authenticity, a documentation of one's values. Saee's desire is to speak a living language, to practice a living architecture—a kind of concretization of living culture that captures and then reveals something new. From the beginning his architecture has been grounded in a dialogue of relationships. His strategies of intervention express the tension between context and container, a tension marked by synthesis and asynchronism. He achieves a momentary equilibrium among all constituent elements of his work without relying on an absolute system of coherence but remaining absorbed in an exploration of laws governing and regulating a method of speaking. Saee's recent work explores surface as the primary ordering device—a continuous deforming surface that acknowledges programmatic constraints and provides coherence yet no longer relies on conventions of repetition, articulation of volumes, or various geometric ordering strategies. In his system, structural and tactile elements are treated with equal importance.

Saee's work is a specific reflection on the increasingly powerful and unavoidable external conditions of our environment. He works by identifying certain traces within the chaotic accumulation of built matter, altering, discriminating, and enhancing them. In this sense his work implies an urban strategy, a tactic of simply improving what already exists. The projects consider context (in the broadest sense) as open possibility. Saee takes enormous pleasure in developing the personality of each new place. This preoccupation with context and his more recent interest in a language derived from analogies to nature, subject to the flows of material and energy, result in an architecture with more animate qualities.

Michele Saee is the prototype of the contemporary nomad. Born in Persia, he later found his way to Italy to work and study in Florence, and then to Los Angeles where I had the pleasure to meet him in 1983. In his two years at Morphosis he had the opportunity to rethink and reconfigure his rationalist mullings with Super Studio and begin a new trajectory more closely oriented to the idiosyncracies and ephemeralities of Los Angeles, a metropolis opaque to the uninitiated. His work transformed quickly after he started his own practice, resonating with the nuanced social, economic, and political realities of this uncertain context (no one would claim this city as an act of will). Saee possesses tremendous innate facility (you can't fake a line) that is quite unfashionable today. He is an architect who must build, and he recognizes that reality proves stranger than anything we could possibly imagine. He pursues his intuition for uncensored ideas, celebrating the transformative possiblities, framing the solution within a sensual context to provoke the discovery of what was formerly unimaginable.

Michele Saee: Imminent Architecture
by Frédéric Migayrou

For Michele Saee, "instances of space" or the instance of space are the principal issues to be identified in his search to define an architecture that rejects an imposed order or example. Each building is an example of instance; it is detailed; it forms a new singularity, a whole that takes shape according to infinitely renewed links. The world is no longer a closed system whose expansion can be controlled, thus, as neither object nor organizing principle can exist, the architect's work must now face an identity crisis. The architectonic has regained its rights, the architect now organizes links and interactions, and each project only appears as a whole at the last moment, or instant.

Michele Saee's architecture provokes a crisis among organized identified elements—be it a crisis of form, of the notion of scheme, of surface, of dwelling, of the closed singularity of the project, its methods of construction, or its engineering. Saee's architecture also embodies a strong temporal dimension. It responds to a Californian tradition of urgency and shelter, to a culture of assemblage and installation. His architecture is of the "instance," propelled by the necessity of time. The instance rejects all metaphors of a unilateral founding moment and is instead an open process. It poses long-standing questions about geometry, permanent resolutions to the scheme, the box, the constraints of partitions and configurations, and the return of hypothetical historical examples both classical and vernacular. It also questions the logic of a project that seeks to differentiate between the language of the architect and that of the engineer, to separate the architectural concept from the technical world.

Saee teaches a true architecture of urgency, an immediate architecture that does not distinguish between the idea and the building. It is an architecture where "instancing" has a generic function: the capacity to mobilize the symbolic, practical, social, and technical aspects of a project to create an exemplary, original built prototype that reinvents the medium and its syntax.

Constituent Arrangement

If one discovers a common understanding of frameworks and screens in Saee's work, it is because these elements have remained a tool for analysis and control that allows him to develop other structural elements quickly. Even the first apartments he designed, 434 Apartments (1986–89), are based on the idea of a cubic volume negatively composed of an assemblage of elements. The study sketches for this project illustrate the various compositions Saee considered in an attempt to approach the series of parallelepiped living spaces differently. Materials are placed to enhance the sense of an arrangement that can always be changed—of an almost unstable assembly. This irresolution introduces the factor of time, the notion of the accidental that remains the determinant in Saee's work. The value of complexity, however, lies beyond just the range of semantic aspects that Robert Venturi attributes to it. In defining a complex system according to Herbert A. Simon as "a large number of parts that interact in a non-simple way,"[1] Venturi advocates a theory based on the element, one that invokes an architecture of composition. The idea of "inflection," which determines the assembly and juxtaposition of the elements, remains the principle influence in Michele Saee's work, but it no longer implies that space is a neutral expanse for the arrangement of elements. Spatiality is prompted by architecture; it is always specific and local, created by this movement of inflection that multiplies, segments, and divides it into so many realms.

Saee's Meivsahna House (1990) perfectly expresses the interrelationship of visual and tactile qualities in his work. Sheets of steel, mobile structures, hanging lights, and laminated panels are all related here at a completely different scale. All of the materials are treated with utmost attention, from the craftsmanlike bent wood to the metal joinery and glass panels. Saee introduces a complex architectural language where space is created through a balance of combined forms; it is an architecture in which drawing takes precedence over composition. Saee resists the industrial norm by evoking Pierre Chareau through an almost craftsmanlike study in which the detail speaks for the whole. Each element is conceived as a designed object that does not leave a definable pattern on the whole building.

Juxtapositions and ambiguity are everywhere in this work, but they cannot be understood as simple collages. The facade of Design Express Warehouse and Furniture Store (1988) is composed of an immense, suspended concrete screen that opens to a rough space, enhancing the refined quality of the furniture on view. The screen also accentuates the relationship between exterior and interior, the building's connection with a surrounding context that the architect wanted to preserve, including the graffiti at the site. The monumental door becomes the allegory of a passageway, the metaphor of access that is both shared by and intrinsic to the idea of image and information. The unity of the building and the form is never assumed; the structure defies the ordering and differentiation of elements.

Elements of a Morphogenesis

Michele Saee's architecture can be interpreted in an almost negative way: the elements form a completely open structure; the drawings delineate something that only exists through a direct experience of space. Exterior synthesis no longer defines the concept; the building resists distinct form and even the notion of identity itself. Moving beyond the radical refusal of the industrial box—an architectural type that is taking over building in California—Saee even seems to reject the idea of connection or articulation that derives from a modern understanding of the scheme. A project like Saee's Trattoria Angeli (1986) is the neo-plasticist evocation of J.J.P. Oud's Café de Unie (1925); it accentuates the idea of a "dis-connection," of traversing planes that highlight materials like metal and glass.

Frameworks, repeated elements, parts of the frame, and supporting structures are present in all of Saee's early projects, but they never restore the unity of abstract space. His first projects with Morphosis express opposition between the building's mass and the displaced metal screen structure, in other words, the transposition of interior and exterior that disrupts one's perception of surfaces and volume. If the facades remain very apparent in the California tradition of emphasizing the image, they also become true sites of transference: an invitation to enter the building, a qualitative exchange between the interior and the street. Saee's search for new architecture originates with mutating scales, the sliding semantic values of signs, vastly enlarged logotypes, and inventing materials and using them in an unorthodox fashion. The giant letters forming the logo on the facade of the Ecru Clothing Store (1988) become true objects. The store window—a blend of facade and name that recalls the blatant California conflation of brand image and roadside billboard—becomes almost an obstacle between the client and the products in the store.

An initial morphological pursuit led Michele Saee to think not only about the formal unity of buildings but also about their entire relationship to engineering and the mechanistic and positivist understanding of the act of construction. In Saee's work the box, the scheme, the layout—all openly challenged—create another type of spatial relation. They form the conditions of a new architectural entity that is completely opposed to the abstract unity of the object or modernist space. The influence of Rudolph Schindler still seems apparent in Saee's will to impose a "local relation," the elementary, sensitive experiences that seem basic to our understanding of material objects.[2] Saee seems to have rediscovered an understanding of form that is similar to the definition of contained consciousness inherited from Gestalt theory, in which form is dependent on structuring, qualitative and geometric relations, and the convergence of objective and subjective factors.

Saee has investigated these issues through various installations and experimental assemblies built around the idea of perception, such as the "proprioception" project at Florida A&M University (1994). The reference to Ronchamps or the allusions to Gaudí in this installation are more about rediscovering a spirit of construction than defining an expressionist understanding of form. Although the drawings may evoke Rudolf Steiner's architecture, the unity of the building does not rely on the sculptural effect of the massing. Behind the obvious forms and sculptural surfaces, Saee attempts to reestablish a concrete human scale—not the universal and abstract measure of the Corbusian body, but a physical presence that inspires contact. The Kantian categories of space and time thus give way to form defined by a relationship of sensorial facts based on a phenomenological understanding of extension and duration. The scheme, the right angle, and the space created by the separations are problematized to favor an assemblage of open spaces.

In the Beverly Hills Cosmetic Dental Clinic (1992), the complex use of floating forms and jutting angles defeats the idea of a scheme. The forms hide multiple openings that admit a mixture of daylight and artificial light to the space. The cold light creates an assembly of autonomous surfaces bisected by fracturing lines that distinguish forms from surfaces, creating zones of varying intensity.

The Disorientated Body, and Finally, Space

This focus on the sensitive links between materials and light should not, however, be compared to the completely phenomenological inspiration of an architect like Steven Holl. For Saee, architecture is not open and perceptive, nor does it involve intentional consciousness or a subject seen within a perspectival order. Rejecting the exteriority of the subject and the logic of representation and projection enforces a relationship to space that is not defined by a point of view, by normalizing an exterior body, or by an appropriate human scale, which was for Alberti and Le Corbusier the measure of geometric space. The fact that the eye no longer orders a normative definition of perspectival space imposes a new relationship on the body and its spatial economy.

For Saee, the body is not normative—an exterior scale that defines rational space. It is no longer the external referent for projected space but is itself projected into space and becomes fragmented and distinct in accordance with continuously repeated spaces.

Saee's reference to the figurative sculpture of traditional African, Buddhist, or Hindu cultures appears to be a morphological tactic. At Ecru Clothing Store, parts of a very stylized Hindu figurine form the contours of the facade, partitions, and elevations. The store is treated as an allegory of the body: the clothing becomes the void—architecture—of a solid anatomy that overwhelms the entire space. A partition inside the store divides like a thoracic cage and the structure becomes a skeleton, creating dynamic and supple space, as in the Angeli Mare restaurant (1990–91). The wood framework inside the restaurant is like the skeleton of a large fish, while a metal cave set on a green parquet floor further enhances the watery dimension.

In Saee's work biomorphic references are never affirmed as such, beyond perhaps historical references to organic forms in the work of Frank Lloyd Wright or Pier Luigi Nervi. Saee's analogies to anatomical form do not rely on the unity of the body as a principle any more than they do on an esthetic of fragmentation, although his research does originate in an esthetic of apportionment, such as fragments of the body chosen for their particular plasticity, and which become the subject of his series of numerous drawings (1989). These drawings, based on historical painting and photography, obliterate the context or ensemble of the body. Yet, through successive erasure, they regain the dynamics of individual limbs, accentuating the strength and morphological singularity of an element of the body suspended in action. Saee takes a radical approach to the phenomenological tenet that a body is divided among a variety of perceptive worlds and that turning these bodily fragments into tools can define a world logic.[3]

If Michele Saee sees clothing as architecture of the body, this vision is reversed when he builds the body into an architectonic element. The body becomes a proportional system imposed like a new template in his buildings; it is a connective tool, an example of a relationship with the outside world. Place is no longer understood as the body's inscription in space, determined by the site and organized by the program. The idea of proximity also changes to signify connection and not vicinity. Real, geometrically measurable space is now only a reference, a parameter at the heart of more complex scales of value.

Henceforth all architecture will be defined as a permanent interrelationship with the world as an open, indeterminate context, and architecture must adapt itself simultaneously to changing evaluations of the world and these contexts. Space is now simultaneously interior and exterior; it no longer controls orientation or hierarchies; it no longer has sides or directions; it is judged differently, according to tensions and balances. Saee's sketches Cardiff Bay (1996), which illustrate numerous fracturing lines, give insight into this methodology.

The Meivsahna House is a container conceived as a structure to which other functions can be added. No box defines spaces and no corridor leads from one room to another. Rather, a change in materials and a sloped and lowered ceiling mark spatial transitions. The floor and ceiling either facilitate or hinder movement, and their interaction can determine the position of a wall, a door, or a passageway, but never in a classical manner. Functions are defined as zones or regions that simply create a demarcation as activity begins. The floors are reached by ramps. As Saee describes the house, it is like a "vase": all of the interior elements work together, and the opening determines the relationships between interior and exterior. Light remains a structural element that defines specific areas. The house is divided into two zones by a central courtyard rather like a continuous line shattering the shell. The idea of clothing, of successive veils constituting a shell for a body, is everywhere. The space appears layered and segmented, its whole impossible to reassemble.

Saee is inventing an architecture that is simultaneous with the world, one that unveils the entire building process and is based on the notion of incompletion. His buildings are not finished; they are not objects or the fruit of an idealistic and formalist project. Finality is no longer represented by form or function: the architect wants to make us accept the accidental, the notion of risk, and the receptive nature of the project. Linkages and organizing zones become the subject of his study sketches, Hides. These are provisional diagrams in which Saee gives his hand free reign, and the resulting generic disorder is preserved as a means of forming space.[4] The installation "Art Works for Children" (1994) incorporates these experiences through drawing and the trait libre, or automatic stroke.

Being an architect not only involves responding to a program and keeping one's distance from an idea or a project, but also making the project effective at all times. The risk is in making architecture that undergoes mutation and permanent transition but that must be simultaneously interpreted and controlled. Michele Saee clears the way for an architecture of morphogenesis and for experimentation with topology, while allowing for unified form through structural stability.[5] However, he never makes this his methodology and does not place the topological figure in geometric space.[6] The Golzari Guest House (1995–96) completely overturns the California typology of a living space set on a slope. Its form seems to swing and slide in almost organic confusion. The diagrams distinguish the axes, but the volumes and spaces are configured so that no scheme ever anticipates the actual form of the building.

Michele Saee attempts to create space using our multiple tools of perception and then to give that space material reality. Architecture becomes an understanding of thresholds: the architect perceives a link with the interface, the in-between of distinct systems, and the "intraface," a term Saee uses. At the intraface, two systems co-occupy space. Architecture of the future thus will have to be not only interactive—fixed in an interaction between two systems—but primarily intra-active. Redefining architectural practice as autopoiesis involves conceiving an architecture without end, beyond the orientation of an arché that is always understood as a retreat. Saee establishes this autonomy and invites us to step into the interface of the virtual, electronic world and the analog, real world. His built architecture is not a shelter, a recessed space, or a simple place for protection: it resembles a prosthesis. It responds to functions that create an interface with the world, and it acts as an instrument of participation.

Saee tries to create experimental spaces, to experiment with place, and to accept the uncertainty of the act of construction. His work does not simply question the whole process of creation or the foundation and methodology of architectural practice as proposed by conceptual architecture. It is more about working without distancing oneself from the project, in a radical "immanence" in which the architect becomes only a vector at the heart of the organizational system. His architecture is authentically modular, to use the classic Phileben term. He creates space by combining dynamic systems—in biological terms, his space is an exogenous symbiosis. Building remains an open process and signifies a template, a possibility, a pattern that must recombine for each project. The combined elements establish a unique order in which space is imminent, where it is "instanced." As Michele Saee would say, the building is the template.

Translated by **Louise L. Rosa**

Notes

1 Robert Venturi, Complexity and Contradiction in Architecture (New York: Museum of Modern Art, 1966), 90.

2 "Schindler's whole conception of architecture rests on the creation of space through the 'local relation' between bodies: This, not function, structure, or building technology— is the crucial determinant. He accordingly described the true modern architect as 'not primarily concerned with the body of the structure and its sculptural possibilities. His one concern is the creation of space forms dealing with a new medium as rich and unlimited in possibilities of expression as any other media of art: colour, sound, mass, etc.'" Lionel March and Judith Seine, R.M. Schindler, Composition and Construction (London: Academy Editions, 1993), 81.

3 "Having a body gives the ability to exercise influence over a 'general organization' of the world from the guise of an intersensorial whole." Arion L. Kelkel, "Le problème de l'intenionalité corporelle," in Maurice Merleau Ponty, Le psychique et le corporel (Paris: Ed. Aubier, 1988), 34. Translation by Louise L. Rosa.

4 Michele Saee, Hides: Sketches of Space (Los Angeles: Public Access Press, 1996).

5 Rene Thom, Structural Stability and Morphogenesis (Boston: Mass., W.A. Benjamin Inc., 1972), 31.

6 Topological understanding of space is most often seen as a formal pursuit, an area of implementation that introduces a new order of thought. This is how Charles Jencks analyzes some of Peter Eisenman's experiments, linking them to an architecture of chaos. Catastrophe is given a metaphoric and suggestive value, but it is not understood as a generative event capable of creating new spatial modulations. See Charles Jencks, The Architecture of the Jumping Universe (London: Academy Editions, 1995).

Forget It :
What the Body Does Best When Left to Itself

by Aris Janigian

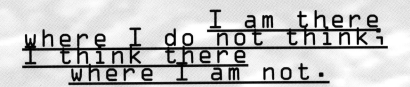

I am there
where I do not think;
I think there
where I am not.

—- Jacques Lacan

In looking at Michele Saee's early work, what strikes me most is the tension that exists between function and play. Saee seems to share the sculptor's joy in shaping material. At the same time, the forms that emerge from this play exist in what I can only describe as a restless balance in relation to their function as walls, counters, and benches. The 100-foot-long facade of Ecru Clothing Store is constructed of slabs of fragmented letters sixteen feet high that spell out ECRU. The idea of the billboard, reflecting the car culture of Los Angeles, was the initial source of inspiration for this facade, but as it developed, another, entirely new source—Paolo Uccello's painting The Battle of San Romano—worked its way into the final form.

That painting pulsates with energy. The bodies of the horses and soldiers fuse into a mass, a composite body, that articulates more a physical than a narrative field. Saee lifts this painting free from its surface and exploits its latent volume and materiality. From the front and back the painting is pulled and extended. Cavities and ruptures emerge, as if the painting were a kind of taffy. A dynamic immediacy, a potential for growth, is realized in the facade. This body, or—given that it is a facade—this really thick skin, is no longer merely a sign, a scrim, or a border-crossing: it is something that communicates in its own right. One has the eerie feeling that if left on its own, the facade might eventually swallow up the street and the patrons inside the store. But it is not left alone. Glass cuts through it, creating openings, like wounds in a body, through which light passes.

With Ecru Marina, Saee takes this impulse to give life to forms even further. The human body was the obvious inspiration for this project. Saee chose, among figures from several cultures and periods, an Indian figurine of the Hindu deity Shiva. From that figurine the sections, elevations, and storefront forms for Ecru Marina were abstracted.

In studying the forms that resulted from this abstraction, however, I cannot decide whether they are meant to be read as stand-ins for the body—that is, symbolic or representational things—or organic, living things. In either case, what is remarkable about this space is how the softness of the lines and the voluptuous curves of the volumes belie their aggressiveness. The sections of the Shiva cut into space as much as Saee cut into her, as if Saee reserved for her the right to someday (re)dress the violation, as though an archaeologist might come upon this site in a thousand years and find the space between these forms gone, a gargantuan Shiva reconstituted from its fragments, tranquilly asleep. All fancy aside, these forms resist being limited to function, and even the bodies of the occupants of this space—the buyers of dresses and trousers—seem insubstantial next to them. Here, as with Ecru Clothing Store, Saee desires to make space palpable, corporeal, and not simply a hollow to occupy.

ALREADY IT IS APPARENT THAT THE BODY IS CRUCIAL TO AN UNDERSTANDING OF SAEE'S WORK. He begins with the body as model or template, but I believe he will go deeper than that and EVENTUALLY IMPLICATE THE BODY OF THE ARCHITECT, HIS OWN BODY, IN THE DESIGN.
The body is a plastic thing-THE BODY OF A BUILDING, THE BODY OF A PERSON, THE BODY OF THE EARTH. The emergence of the medical and penal disciplines that Michel Foucault has charted as a new discourse, advances in technology, and genetic engineering have the effect of making the body transparent and at the same time extending it. As these bodies are extended, traversed by forces that are foreign to them, THEIR IMAGE OF INTERNAL INTEGRITY IS VANISHING. WE ARE AWARE AS NEVER BEFORE OF THE DEGREE TO WHICH BODIES ARE CAUGHT UP IN A BREAKDOWN—NOT THE BREAKDOWN THAT COMES FROM TORTURE, BUT THAT WHICH COMES FROM MULTIPLE EXPOSURES. Rather than reflecting reality, discourse is shown to be a plastic power that shapes not only what we see, but the organ that sees. DISCOURSE, IN A WAY, BECOMES MATERIAL. In another context, Wallace Stevens said of a poem,

"It can kill a man."

But back to the body.

What the mind has always tried to do is keep the body from giving out on it, to stall its dissolution-SOMETHING WE HAVE DONE VIRTUALLY AND MIGHT ONE DAY SUCCEED IN ACTUALLY DOING. The cloning of animals is a step in this direction, and one suspects that human cloning is, however inappropriate, also inevitable. Another layer is added with cyberspace, where "disembodied" bodies might someday make the constraints of time and space obsolete. THESE DEVELOPMENTS CORRELATE WITH THE SHAKING DOWN OF HEAVEN —and the intuition that perhaps the body that Paul promised us on earth did not require the Messiah's return.

Even before we began to toy with setting the body free in deed, Freud and Nietzsche had begun to set the body free in thought. FOR FREUD, THE BODY IS THE FIRST AND MOST IMPORTANT THING —EVERYTHING ELSE FOLLOWS. The ego develops from the splitting of the joy of the body from the body. In this split, an ideal body is set up, against which the unruly, absent-minded body that we possess has little to recommend itself. IT SHIRKS EXTERNAL RESPONSIBILITY AND IS A THREAT TO STABILITY, TO CIVILIZATION. In order for the id to get what it wants, it requires the aid of the ego. The ego makes the body function in an economy and gives it a certain use-value, a meaning outside of itself: what Freud called the "reality principle." Various utopian scenarios, like that painted by Norman O. Brown, call for a return to the body, its play and its pleasures, a revolution against the reality principle that keeps it in check. But Brown and his ilk fail to acknowledge the risk of giving the body over to itself; THEY DO NOT RECOGNIZE THE ANXIETY THAT COMES FROM ITS FLOATING FREE IN AN INDEFINITE ECONOMY.

The architect is virtually glutted with the reality principle, criss-crossed with contingencies, caught between the life of pure play and the life of the contract in all its manifestations, from the economic to the social to the personal. Mindful of these contingencies, the architect, more than the artist, makes compromises—his or her ego must remain involved. At the risk of further conflating conceptual schemes, I RECALL HEIDEGGER, WHO WOULD SAY THAT ARCHITECTS MUST "FORFEIT" THEIR AUTHENTICITY in order to meet the will of the "they" and keep the machinery moving.

 Angeli Mare is a good example of this tension between function and play in Saee's work. As with the two Ecru stores, here he is concerned with setting things in motion either through cuts and contours or by playing with material to create volumes. However, this space seems to submit to function more so than the two Ecrus. There is a visceral distance from the material, and a formal, representational quality to the space—a desire on Saee's part to give a sense of place. Even so, one does have the feeling of BEING INSIDE OF SOMETHING THAT CAN BREATHE, and now and then—as is the case with the Angeli Mare wine rack, which has a half-comic ponderousness about it LIKE THE IRONY OF AN ELEGANT CIRCUS ELEPHANT—THE FORM BECOMES DOMINANT. Saee seems to struggle between giving himself over to the material fully and returning like a wayward child to the role he was assigned as architect. He still has not used his body to cut, he still has not put his own body on the rack. In this way, the Beverly Hills Cosmetic Dental Clinic becomes a transition point, or rather, a dropping off point. One has a hard time thinking of an environment that is more excruciatingly functional than a dentist's office. Yet Saee designs a very intimate space, aware of the body in every particular—from the material to the scale of the design, as though he saw himself squirming in the choke-hold of that dental chair, or perhaps peering into the soft flesh of the mouth. Here, the body is no longer the inspiration for the design but a measure, in at least two senses of that word: the gauge of the design's fitness or goodess, and the physical reference point (or measuring stick) for the design.

After this point Saee turns his attention to two projects — "proprioception" and "Art Works for Children"—THAT ARE A RADICAL BREAK FROM HIS USE OF THE BODY as either measure of or model for the design. FOR THREE YEARS HE STRUGGLED TO PRODUCE A DESIGN THAT WOULD BE CLOSER TO HIS OWN SKIN, that resisted being reduced to a mere commodity. After numerous aborted attempts, he finally picked up a sketchbook and began to let his hand move freely over the page. The designs for the two projects above were born from this exercise, this play.

GEORGES BATAILLE observed that the world of work, with its emphasis on utility, progress, building, and storing things up is antithetical to the deepest human needs. For Bataille, work degrades humans and relegates them to the order of things. IT IS ONLY WHEN HUMANS ACT PROFITLESSLY, WITHOUT REGARD FOR TOMORROW, THAT THE "ARCHITECTURE OF THE SELF" COLLAPSES AND JOY, OR WHAT BATAILLE CALLED "INTIMACY," IS EXPERIENCED, HOWEVER BRIEFLY. The exuberant movement of Saee's hand across the page is a manifestation of this intimacy. He does not simply refract the body and material into so many functional assignments. He gives the material up to the body, and he gives the body up to the material. DIRECTLY. He is no longer designing, no longer managing from the outside, but WORKING FROM THE INSIDE, as it were. THE BODY IS TWISTING FREE OF ITS FUNCTIONALITY. IT IS FREEING ITSELF FROM A DEFINITE ECONOMY.

As Saee tells it, something unexpected and disturbing happened after "proprioception" was finished. When work began, the site was to take the shape of a symmetrical cross, but when it was completed and photographed from overhead, it became apparent that the digging had transformed the land into the shape of a Christian cross. This was a university whose student population was 80 percent African-American. People feared that gasoline would be poured into the site and set aflame, either by the Ku Klux Klan or in keeping with their example. Saee's relations with the Florida A&M University administration soured when he refused to alter the project. They fenced off the site, and within two months it was completely abandoned and destroyed.

ARCHITECTS ARE SLAVES TO FUNCTION. The site, program, economy, and especially bodies other than the architect's own are all kinds of snares. The way in which this object of play—born of the body—lies inside a cross is as telling as it is accidental. What was Christ's body if not the ultimate compact between the reality principle and the self-identical joy of play? The body must have its joy inside a crucifix; it must, in a way, pay a price for calling itself the "I am who I am."

I believe that risk and anxiety have been salient in Saee's work from the "proprioception" project on. One wonders what might have emerged if something as big as a building could have been marked by the body. Still, the model of the Golzari Guest House gave him an opportunity to move in this direction. The model resulted from many months of ripping and tearing pieces of paper and layering them in a queasy equilibrium. It seems that Saee simply quit the project rather than finished it, as though he could have ripped and tore into it forever.

Saee rejoices in this ripping, the way a dog goes at newspaper with his teeth, his whole body, and then walks away in proud forgetfulness. BUT HUMANS ARE TRAPPED BY THEIR PURPOSEFULNESS, THEIR BACKGROUND, THEIR MEMORY. Memory is a mechanism that directs our moves beforehand and organizes the consequences of those moves into patterns, what psychologists call schemata. These are functional in that they make the past interpretable, allow for the prediction of the future, and ground the present. Conversely, play wants to escape its own ground. Forgetting— what the body does best if left to itself—comes to the foreground in this period of Saee's work. Nietzsche associates the raw life of the body with forgetting. FORGETTING OPENS UP THE HORIZON OF POSSIBILITIES: it is an active move to limit the presence of the past; to wash away the debt. We will debt in order to escape play, to escape our provisionality. This is the seduction of the contract.

THE RISK OF THE AUTHOR IS CLEAR in the Golzari project. The drama of the model (if we can call it that anymore) is its play. Each gesture is like a Nietzsche dice throw. The body of the author enters into an indefinite skirmish with materials in an open field. The tension here is between the will for a ground and the urge to play. Ground is the question posed by the piece itself. Or maybe, the absence of a ground is the ground.

WE ARE REMINDED, ONCE AGAIN,

THAT THE DECENTERING OF THE SUBJECT IS NOT AUTOMATIC.

IT HAPPENS TO US IN MEASURE WITH OUR LABORS; THE RISK WE TAKE

IN KEEPING OPEN THE CORPUS OF OUR WORK.

[

1986

Trattoria
WEST LOS ANGELES
Angeli]

Trattoria Angeli, the second in a series of three important restaurant collaborations with chef and owner Evan Kleiman, began at Morphosis with Angeli Caffé on Melrose Avenue (1984). It was there that the issues of a billboard facade first surfaced and were recognized. This facade treatment was again considered for the Trattoria but developed one step further. Where the first facade had no interaction with the existing building except in its structural connections, the billboard of the Trattoria was integrated with the building itself so the facade became a structural element in the design. Diners are partially screened from the traffic of Santa Monica Boulevard but also interact with the street through a disengaged facade and a window that provides only glimpses of the sky and passersby: feet and bodies passing the small openings between the facade and the building.

Because the surrounding area provided nothing in the way of historical context, the building itself, a former carpet outlet, became the conceptual link to the idea of the traditional Italian trattoria that inspired this project. The use of rusticated brick and bow trusses lends an aged quality to the building that suggests reuse rather than new structure. Turning the focus of history on the building itself meant addressing the concept of integration.

...How can a project express(place)...without resorting to the basic symbolism of rice paper lamps, simple tatami mats, or fishing nets full of shells ?

...Angeli Trattoria project does not literally transfer symbols, materials, or atmosphere- it thinks of the foreign restaurant as if it already were "Angelized" and so creates a contamination for interiors which in all probability will become a genre in the years to come."

- Manolo De Giorgi
Domus January 1989

Everything about the warehouse suggested the stage: acoustics, lighting, the vaulted ceiling with its open bow trusses—even its previous function as a carpet outlet, where hundreds of different carpets suggested costume and concealment, each pattern telling a story. The warehouse thus became a theater for the act of dining, something to be viewed and responded to. Sitting and eating were transformed into a relationship between audience and drama: This restaurant, based more on interaction than on subjective performance, has its "stage" near the center of the main space, in the form of the food preparation area and pizza oven, to facilitate that interaction and to enhance the theatrical mood.

The Trattoria's major elements were fabricated at a steel workshop, transported to the site, and "plugged in" to the existing building. Thus construction was not burdened by the natural elements or restricted or influenced by the site: it occurred within a vacuum. The steel fabricator, protected in his own environment, needed only to follow the working drawings; he was not burdened with the task of foreseeing the application of the steel. Had he been working on site, the design of the pieces might have been altered as questions of application arose. Consequently, the pieces finally delivered to Trattoria Angeli did not plug in as easily as one would have wished; it required time and labor to make them work. The existing Douglas fir bow trusses were left exposed and Douglas fir became the

wood of choice throughout the restaurant, in plywood panels behind the Cor-Ten facade, in the walls of the second-floor dining area, and in the wainscoting of the main space.

In this case, the plug-in philosophy had less to do with the building template than with the existing language of the site that was considered valuable enough to serve as a catalyst for design.

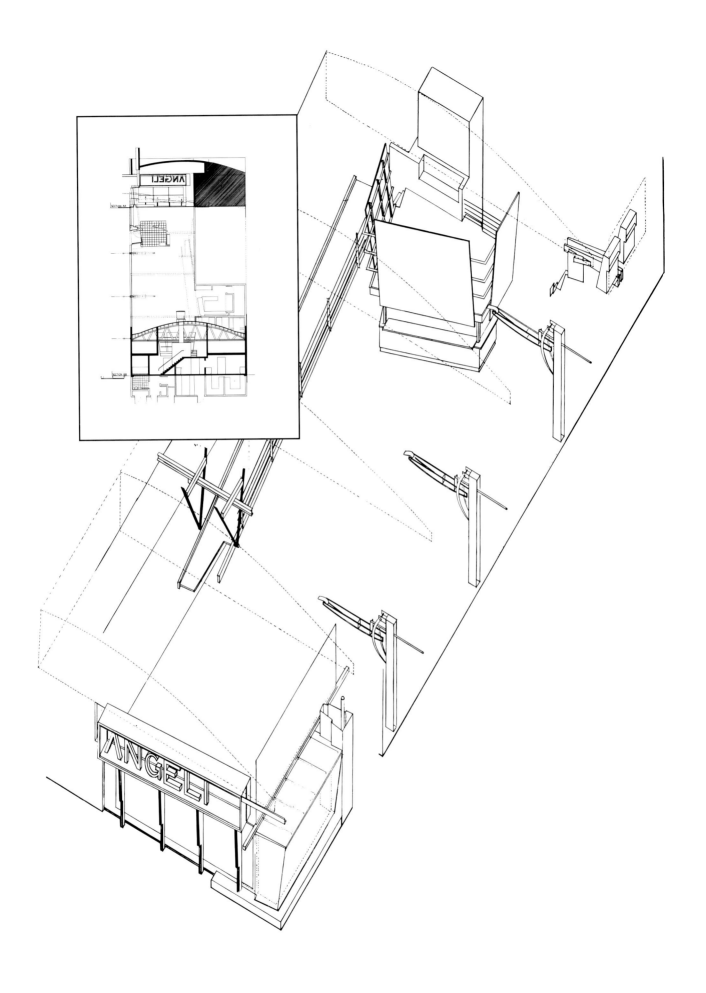

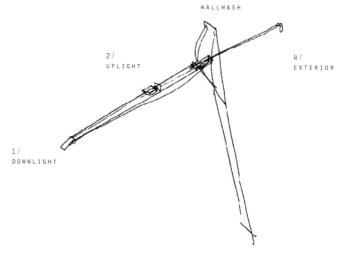

3/
WALLWASH

2/
UPLIGHT

4/
EXTERIOR

1/
DOWNLIGHT

[
434
Apartments]

The 434 apartment complex

marked the break from Morphosis and the first major project for the new firm, Building. This 20-unit complex uses the lot number 434 as a guide for the southern components of the structure: four duplex units, three first-floor gardens, four rooftop gardens.

The lot lies just west of Hoover Street, a north-south artery that separates the checkerboard layout of the city grid to the west from the less-structured response to the radical topography of downtown Los Angeles to the east. This complex was inspired by the housing developments of the 1920s and 1930s in the nearby Echo Park neighborhood, which consist of individual units, almost cabins, separated by open main and branch corridors built into a hillside.

The typical multi-family apartment house is characterized by lack of cross-ventilation, insufficient light, and little or no contact with neighbors or the outside. In breaking away from that type to create a more desirable, comfortable living situation, we discovered that those qualities were the result of a code-driven design; altering them often produced building code violations. As a result, applying for variances was an ongoing process; altering the design, the construction, and the materials to produce a code-sufficient building became a hallmark of the project.

The high-level precision and craftsmanship that characterize Ecru and Angeli Mare were first introduced at 434 and applied to the basic construction principles.

The complex so nearly exceeded the limits of existing building codes that any deviations in the accuracy of construction would have required additional time and money and threatened the life of the project. Because the initial framing was 1/2 inch off, foreseeing problems with sheathing, drywall, and other applications became a necessary skill.

The design and eventual construction of the building became a singular investment in time and energy. Managing all the tasks required to realize one project—arranging financial backing and management, selecting and purchasing the site, obtaining the permits, and meeting building requirements—produced the confidence necessary to push the limits in subsequent projects.

The imposing south wall generates the overall form. Emerging from that wall is a large continuous structure that forms the core of the complex. From there the structure separates, creating a large open corridor; then it divides to form the three open courtyards and four individual duplexes.

While the design of the complex resists the influence of typical apartment housing, it is sympathetic to the surrounding context of single-family homes. The large south wall is sheathed with the same asphalt shingles that cover many nearby houses. The tenants can move freely about outside the individual apartments, much as one can in the yard of a house.

The facade is designed to conceal the building's multi-unit function, with a curved steel wall that both shields and gestures to the entrance. A small-scale window reduces the building's impact as it rises above the curving facade, while open corridors project past the face of the building to the street.

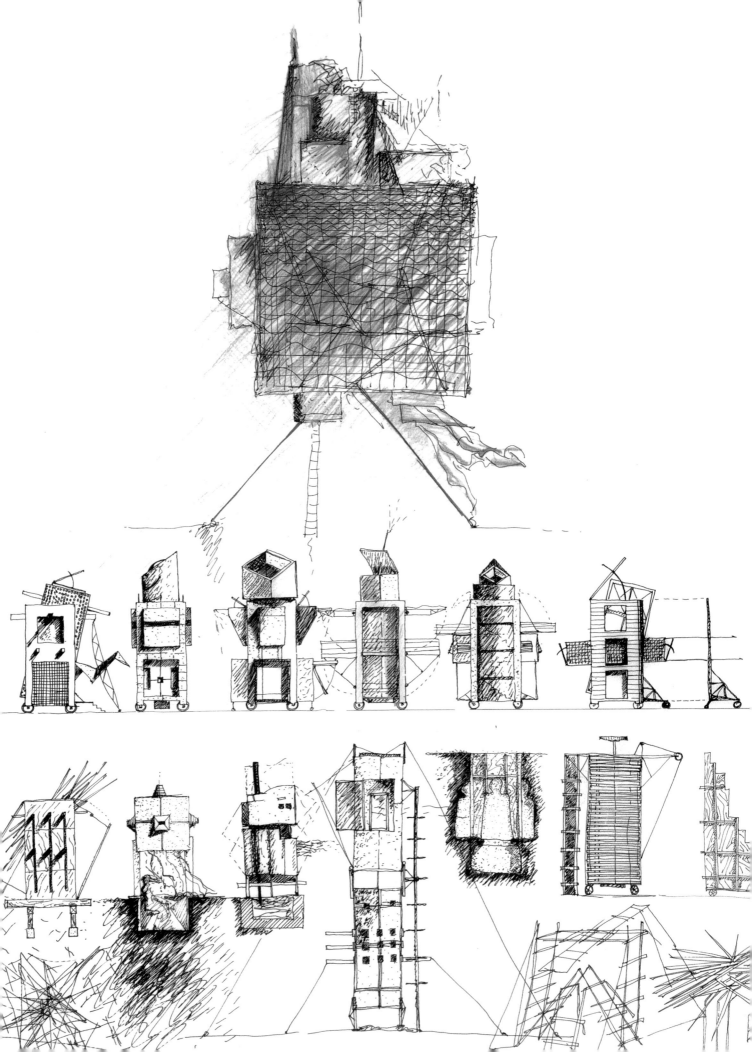

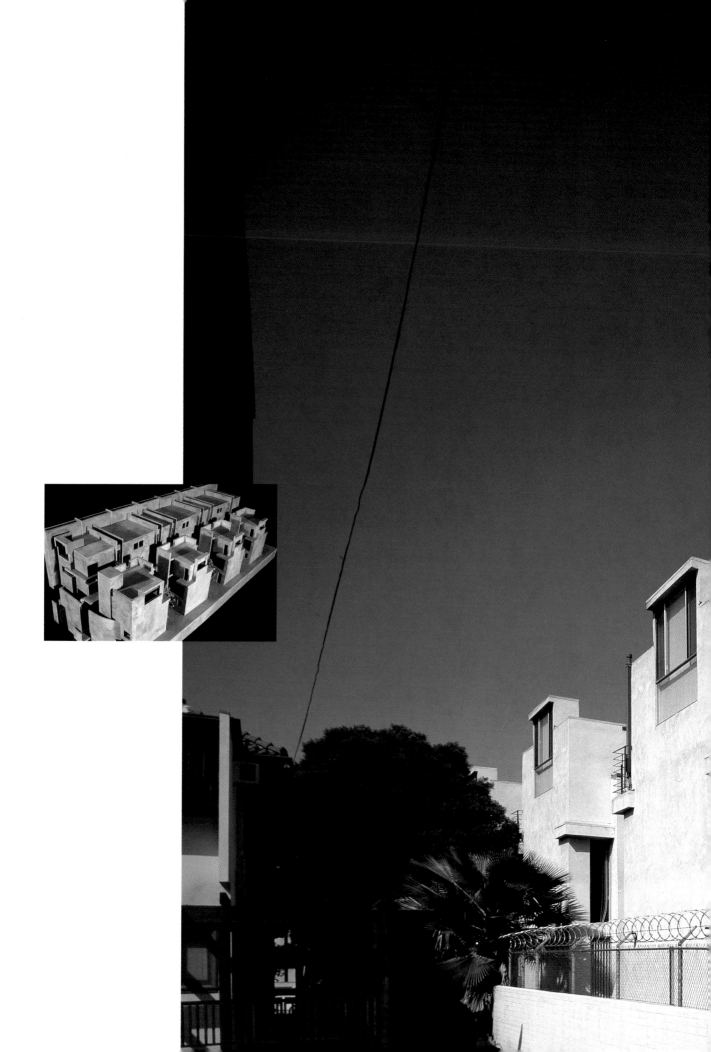

[

Sprecher House

]

This remodel of a 1945 one-story tract house in the Pacific Palisades area of Los Angeles included a major two-part addition. The additions rely on and use portions of the existing house to define the new spaces, but they also appear to resist the old house. The first addition is a single-story curved volume that wraps the long, narrow, south side of the house and "crashes" into it. This positive collision creates a new bathroom, additional space for the kitchen, and a closet for the master bedroom.

The second addition is a second level over the master bedroom. The piece is integrated with the rear of the house and the volume of the bedroom to form a high-ceilinged cube. A central corridor runs lengthwise through the house and becomes a main spine that begins to the east at the main entry and front landing and terminates to the west at the swimming pool. In this corridor people are moving continually and making decisions on the run; while spaces of rest, contemplation, and gathering are found off the spine.

N

1

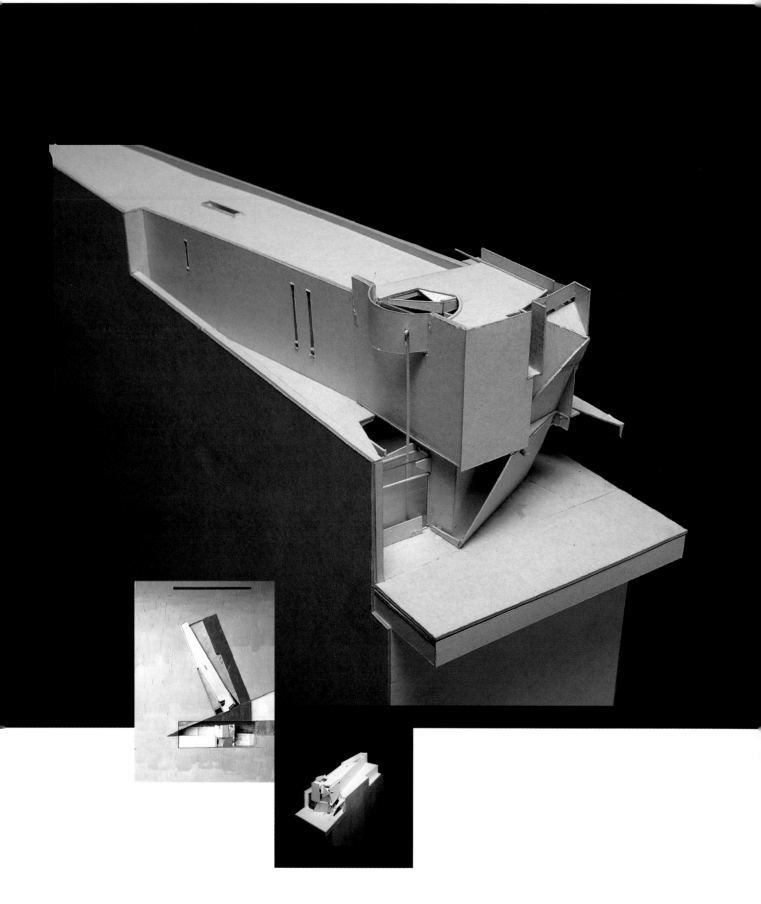

Capitaine Restaurant

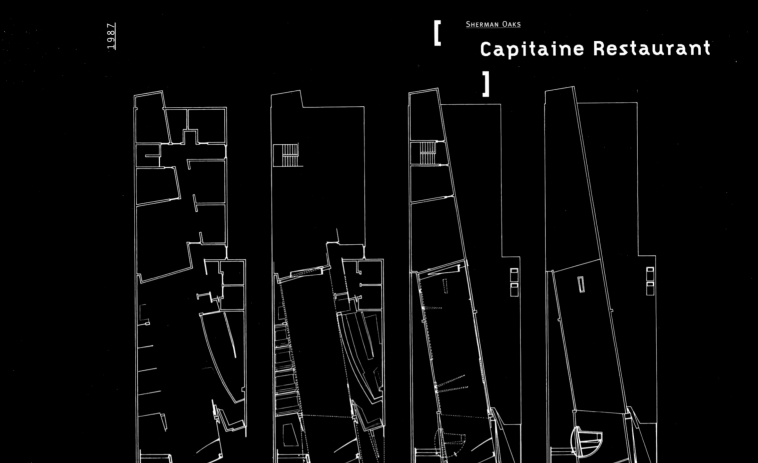

Japan in the seventeenth century opened its seaports to maritime explorers and treasure hunters.

Men of the sea went to this land of mystery to explore new terrain, markets, and products.

In the process they recreated their own image and subculture in the old land.

In the twentieth century a group of Japanese businessmen came to Los Angeles to create a unique version

of what they know as the myth of the Capitaine.

Expressed in a restaurant setting, this myth explores the place where

a sea captain went to eat and entertain.

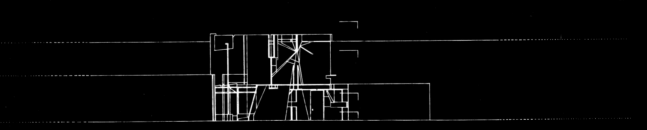

" The man of the sea

<u>Capitaine</u>

The man of science"]

In the Capitaine Restaurant the notion of plugging in to an existing building was pushed to the limit by applying new volumes that appear to literally rest on top of the building. The facade is meant to hide the building's true nature like a mask or the expression of a classic Noh actor. Customers enter not from the front but from the side of the building. Just inside, an oculus-skylight immediately engages the customer's attention, and light focuses the view toward a long, needlelike central corridor. This volume is flanked by a bar on the right and intimate dining booths on the left. The main dining space lies between the two and acts as a central stage.

The mask that is first encountered at the street facade finally drops away at the end of the corridor, where a window exposes the kitchen. Here nothing is hidden: in the kitchen the existing building is revealed and the guts of the structure are put on display, including the plumbing and gas and electrical lines. This is the real face of the building behind the mask.

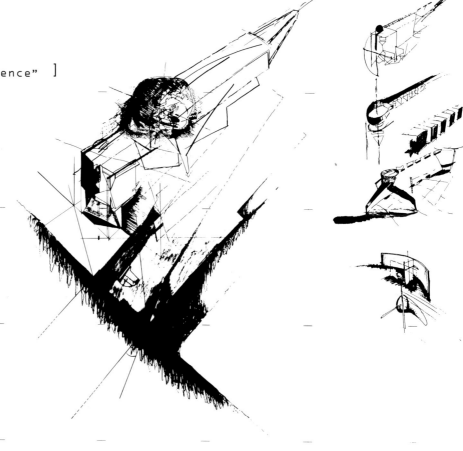

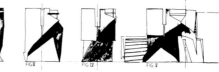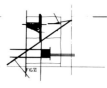

FIG I   FIG II   FIG III   FIG IV   FIG V   FIG VI

<u>The young man awoke</u> in the silence of sleeping space.
   He heard the whispering of people arriving
   like the water coming to the shore.

<u>The sound attracted him</u>, reminding him of his other
life.
   He walked through a cold entrance of steel and
   wood into a tall and spacious area.
   He felt he was in the brain of another man.

<u>He looked up</u>, and through the semicircular / rectangular
   skylight he saw the full moon.

<u>It illuminated</u> the interior space.
   He continued down the tall, narrow
   space towards the source of the
   noise.

<u>The light falling</u> on the pattern of the wood
   floor created separate
   areas which were like the different
   stages in his mind.
   He reached a window that looked
   into another space.

<u>Its shiny surfaces urged</u> him to enter.
   Little by little he became slower and
   finally, motionless, he landed on the
   stainless surface.

<u>He discovered the stars above</u>

<u>And for the first time</u> looked into
   the face of the night.

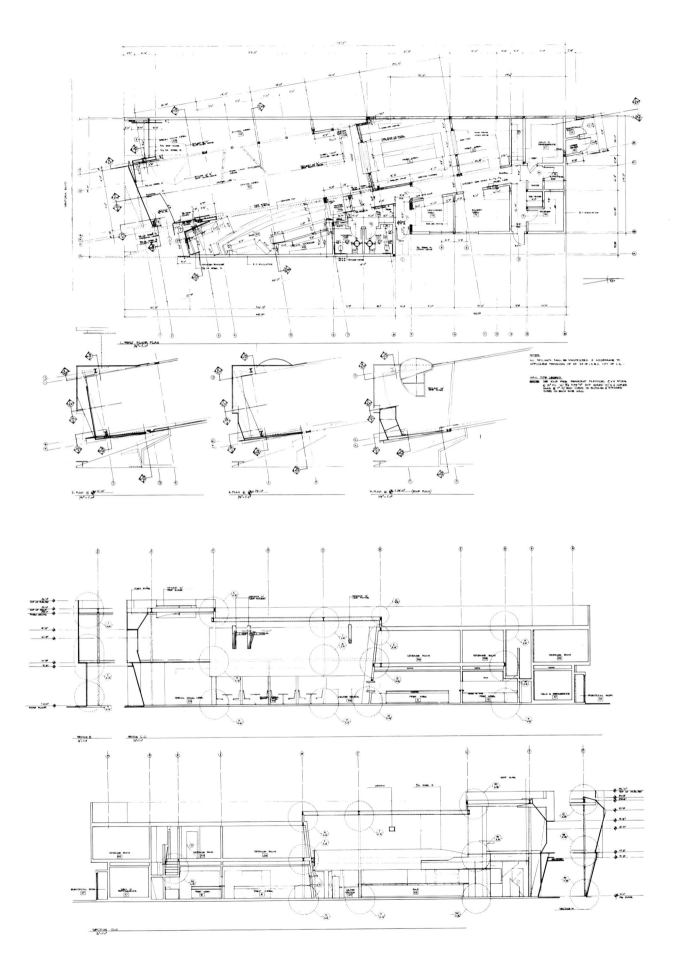

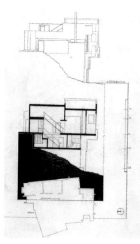

This house on a hillside overlooking Laurel Canyon is named after the street in Germany where the owner was born, tying it to a home of the past, a home of memory. Thus the site had a presence, a sense of place, before any construction took place.

The house's materials reflect its earthen quality: a wood-frame wall of plaster cement, steel frame windows, wood doors, and a concrete floor. The design responds to the slope with three main elements placed at different levels and heights: a dominant east wall, the main body of the house, and a two-car garage to the west. This staggered combination of wall, main volume, and storage ends in the living room, where a single large window opens to a view of Laurel Canyon. The client owned another house to the east that he wanted to keep well separated from the new house. The east wall not only provided a necessary screen but became a structural element that could be built onto or carved into. Narrow slits of windows penetrate each bedroom except one, in which a window projects from the east wall and affords a view of the canyon.

The position of the house takes full advantage of the canyon views, provides a sense of connection with the earth, and creates a circulation pattern that follows the downward slope of the hillside. Because the street is extremely narrow, the garage was placed on an angle to facilitate access and parking.

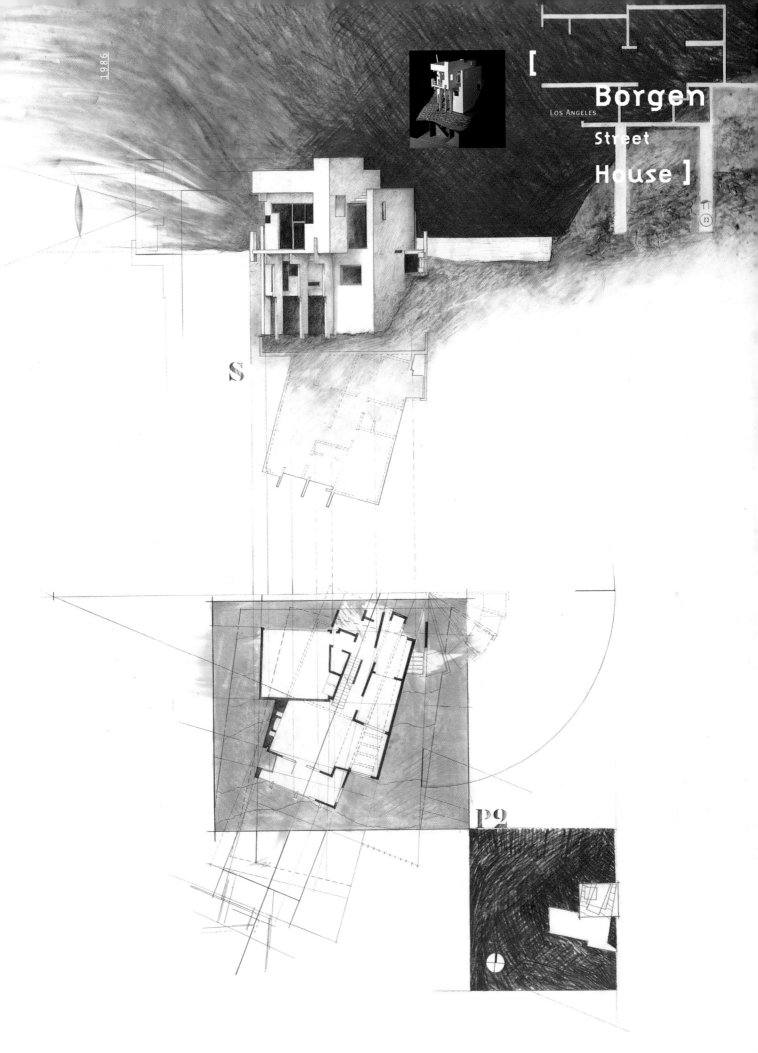

1986

LOS ANGELES

[**Borgen**
Street
House]

S

P2

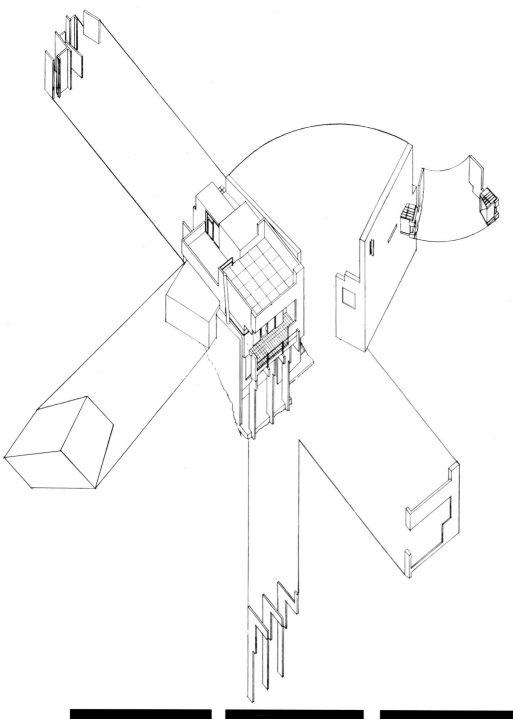

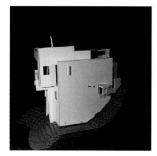

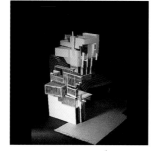

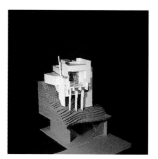

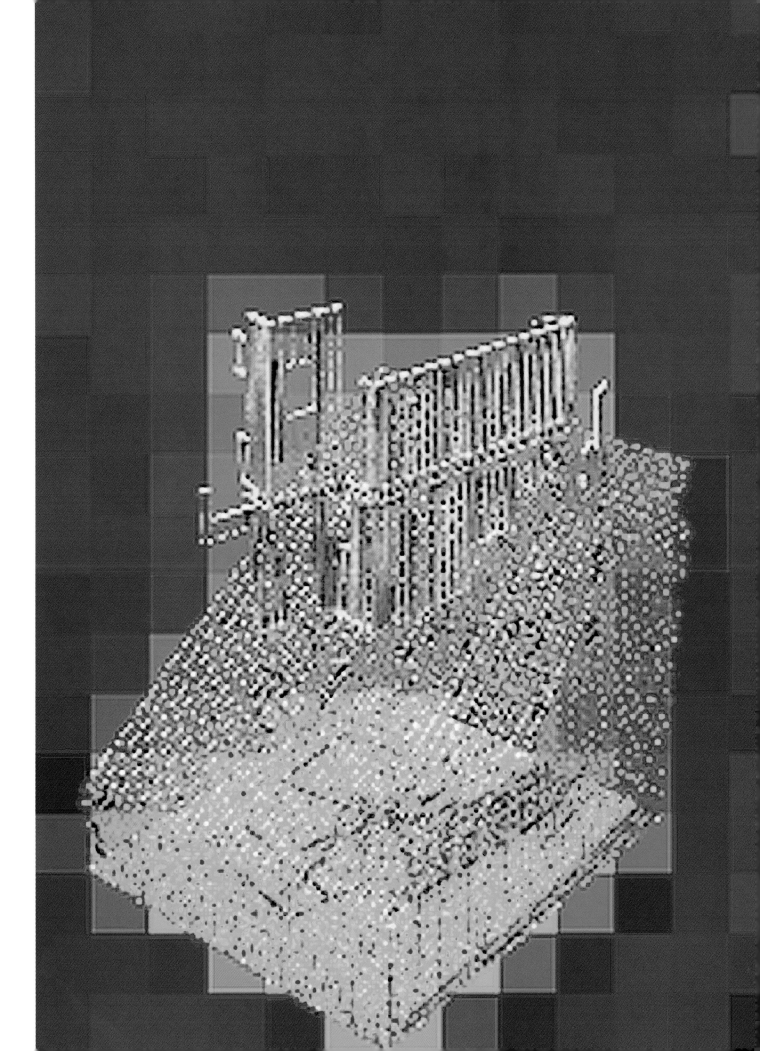

In designing this remodel and addition to a 1930s house we felt it was important to remember and understand the history of the existing structure. The old house was leaning because its foundation and termite-infested walls were crumbling. The traces of the building spoke of a weak beginning and years of neglect hidden by layers of colorful wallpaper and paint. This was an exhausted body deprived of its dignity.

Contrary to some of Building's other projects, which have been about placing a container within another container, this house is constructed on top of and beyond the footprint of the original house. The space of the future does not exist without the memory of the past. The role of memory in architectural spaces is fundamental to the degree that one can feel it with all of the senses.

The skin of the house was removed, the skeleton was lifted, and new foundations were poured. The new volume replaced, added to, and transformed the existing configuration to respond to the client's growing family, who demanded more autonomy and larger quarters. On the first floor the house was extended six feet to the east and west, which dramatically changed the living and dining space. The bookshelves along the north wall accommodate a large collection while allowing light to penetrate through the crevasses of long, narrow steel windows with arm extensions that support the shelves.

New custom-designed, steel pivoting doors created an inside/outside space, the new deck addition toward the courtyard. An existing staircase leads to the second floor, where the new centralized bathroom tower uses an ancient cooling method, wind, to circulate moist air through the house. It is quiet and respectful. The additional room over the garage extends into a balcony, toward a beautiful old oak tree; a ladder leads to the roof garden, with a 360-degree view.

[ᴮᴿᴱᴺᵀᵂᴼᴼᴰ Chapman Jones ¹⁹⁸⁸
House]

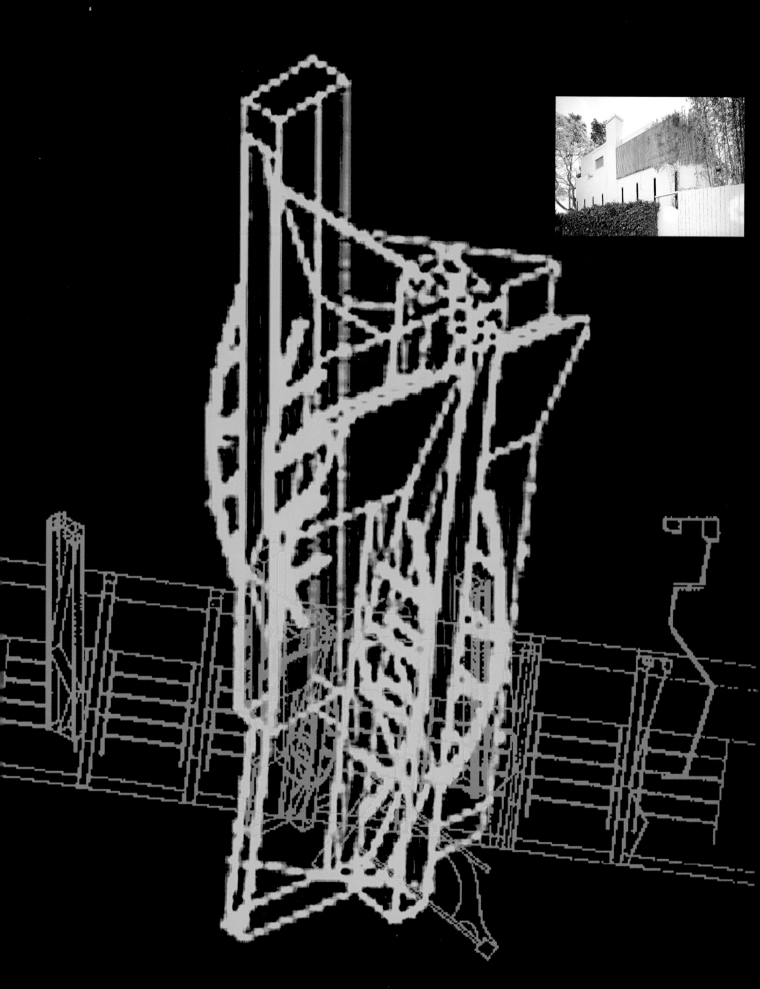

Ecru Clothing Store]

LOS ANGELES

The first Ecru, a high-end clothing boutique on Melrose Avenue that closed in 1992, was an experiment in understanding the relationship between urban Los Angeles and the typical retail store and how they connect at the curb. The idea of the facade as a billboard of sorts, first introduced in the Angeli restaurants, was abstracted for Ecru, whose sign explored the dynamic elements of perception. The facade was designed to be viewed through the windshield of a car. The sign was never able to be viewed the same way twice: traffic rules did not allow it, nor did the driver's personal safety. As the viewer accelerated past the facade it metamorphosed, and when one finally closed in on it, it became illegible. How does one perceive a thing that cannot be read from a distance of six feet but only from the driver's seat of a speeding car one hundred yards away?

R

E

C

The letters that formed the facade derived from a standard lettering template. The essence of each of the letters was extracted from the template, so there was no waste. The design team wanted something very recognizable to the passerby, but it did not want a billboard in the typical sense, so the letters were constructed minimally with only enough form to allow them to be perceptible. The result represented the evolution of the lettering template or a fracturing of the type. Together the lettering and the facade consti-tuted not a simple overlay but a marriage of the two, layering in the finest sense. At times the facade was dominant; at other times, the letters.

The Ecru facade also drews from an element of L.A. culture that is less tangible than the car: the mural. The mural is an attempt to stabilize the overhang-ing L.A. environment by applying a history, a layer of something well explored and familiar, to the face of something new and foreign. While it resembles the bill-board in scale, its message is quite the opposite. The mural's intent is to provoke memory, to capture and reinforce the past; while the billboard is primarily concerned with the present. At Ecru these ideas converged in the facade. The partial lettering suggested a decay, a process; while its steel construction established a sense of permanence in a city that appears temporary. The facade created an ambiguous history for the building that dis-guised the structure's true "plug-in" nature.

E C R U

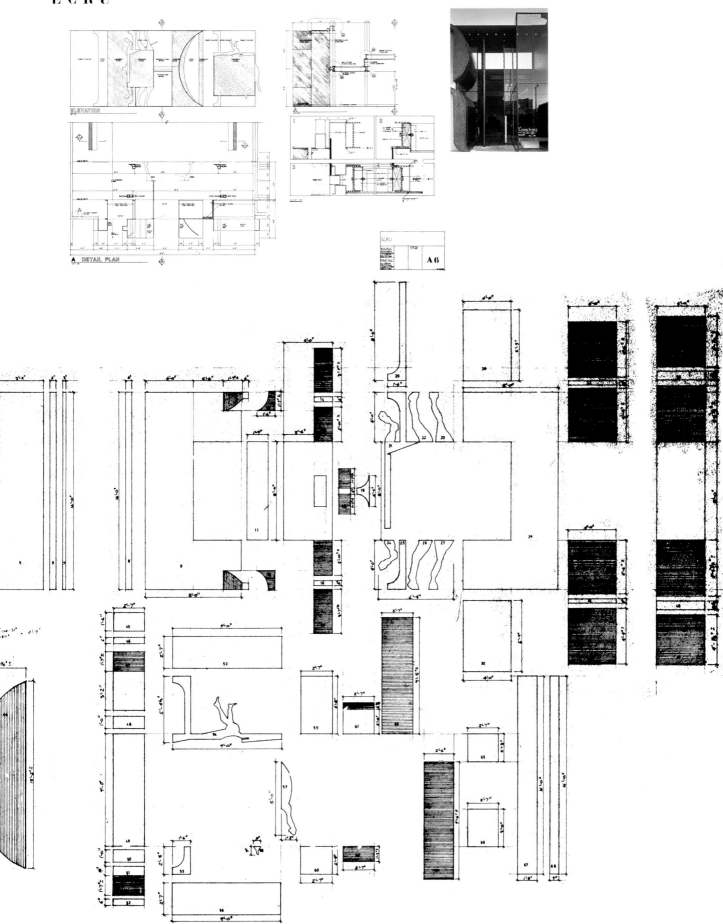

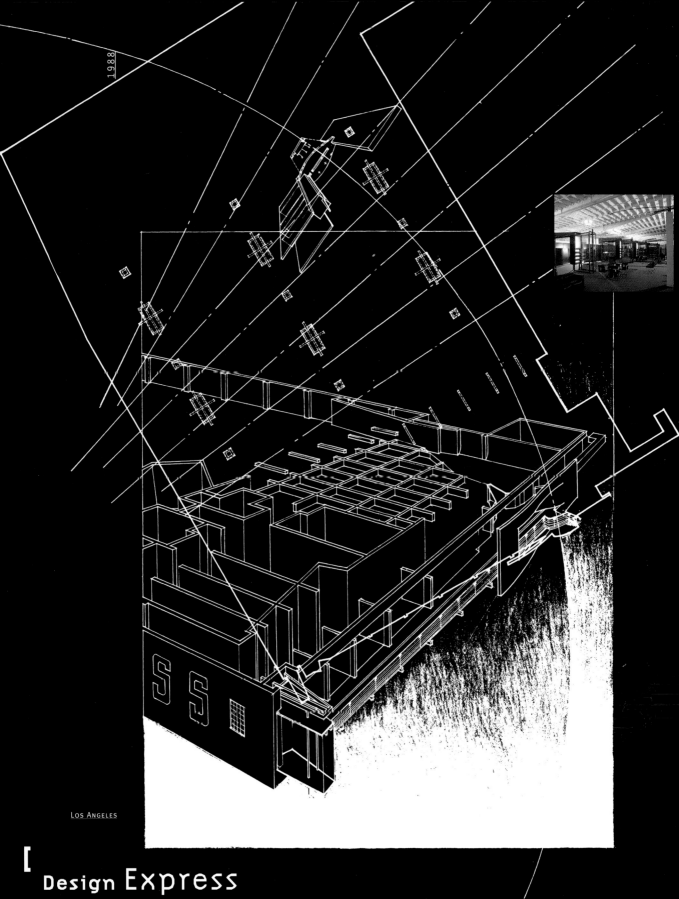

1988

LOS ANGELES

[
Design Express
Warehouse and Furniture
Store]

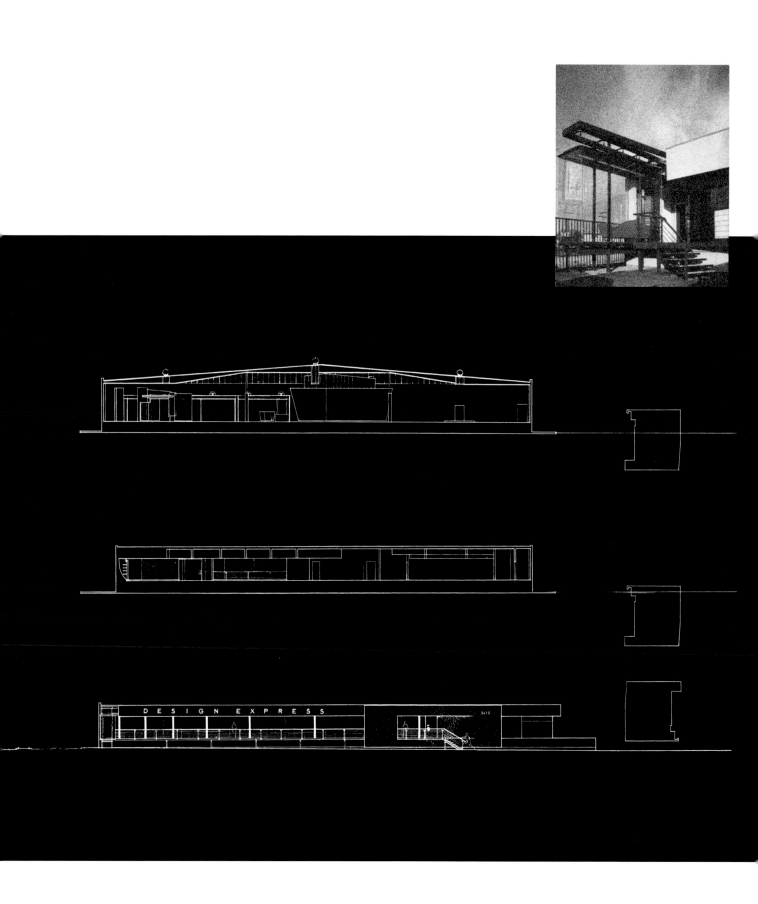

DESIGN EXPRESS

Design Express

is a contextual work that relies on both the contrast and the complementary relationship between building and merchandise to deliver its message, that a retail space can be injected into an industrial context.

This was a container-within-a-container project. The building is a 55,000-square-foot former Plexiglas fabrication warehouse in an industrial zone. The large scale of the structure did not work well with the human-scaled furniture inside that was its focus. While some aspects of the building's industrial history were highlighted in the design, others had to be altered to produce an affable relationship between merchandise and structure. The cold industrial space was humanized by emphasizing a progressive reduction in scale as one approaches the building, moving from the scale of the city to that of the parking area, then to the more intimate interior.

Sporadically used railroad tracks lie just east of the building, street traffic is heavy, and graffiti remains on the building's facade, creating a mildly hostile environment. The floor of the structure was forty-two inches above grade, a carryover from its industrial past that was immediately viewed as an obstacle because a raised floor is normally a hindrance to the casual pedestrian. However, once design began the raised floor became an opportunity: it enhances the billboard effect of the glass showcases along the facade, fully visible above the parked cars. The raised floor also physically separates the building from its industrial surroundings and the noise and rush of traffic. A steel staircase leads to a large glass display case projecting from the facade that marks one of two entrances. A catwalk takes customers past the glass facade and steel walls

that create display spaces to an 8-by-12-foot door that opens partially, creating a crack in the concrete building.

The distinct contrast between the ragged industrial landscape and the polished furniture inside the building further enforces the notion of protection and comfort. The precision and machinelike quality of some of the furniture corresponds to the building's history, while the comfort symbolized by other furniture pieces eases the harshness associated with the warehouse structure.

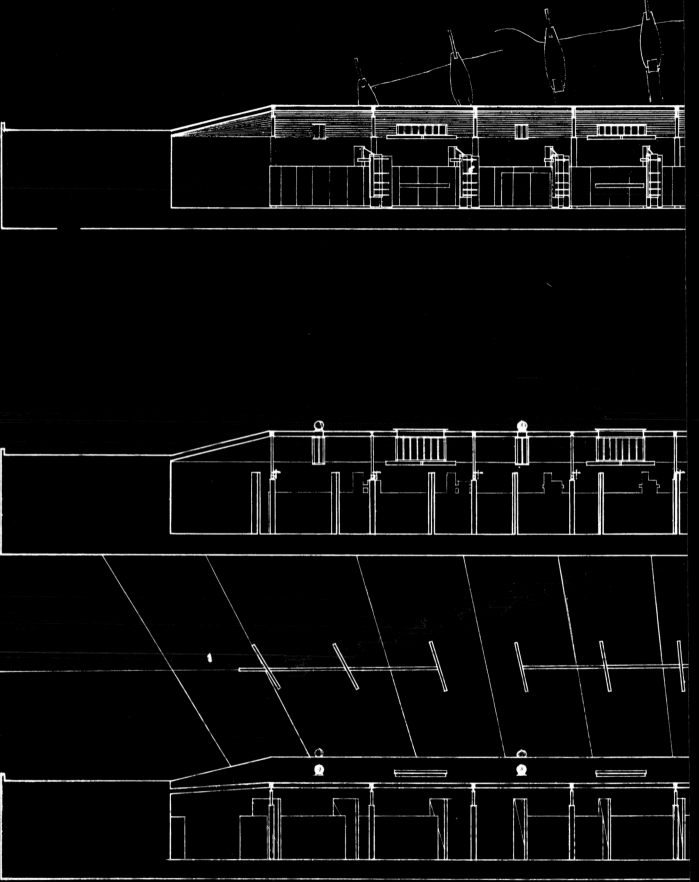

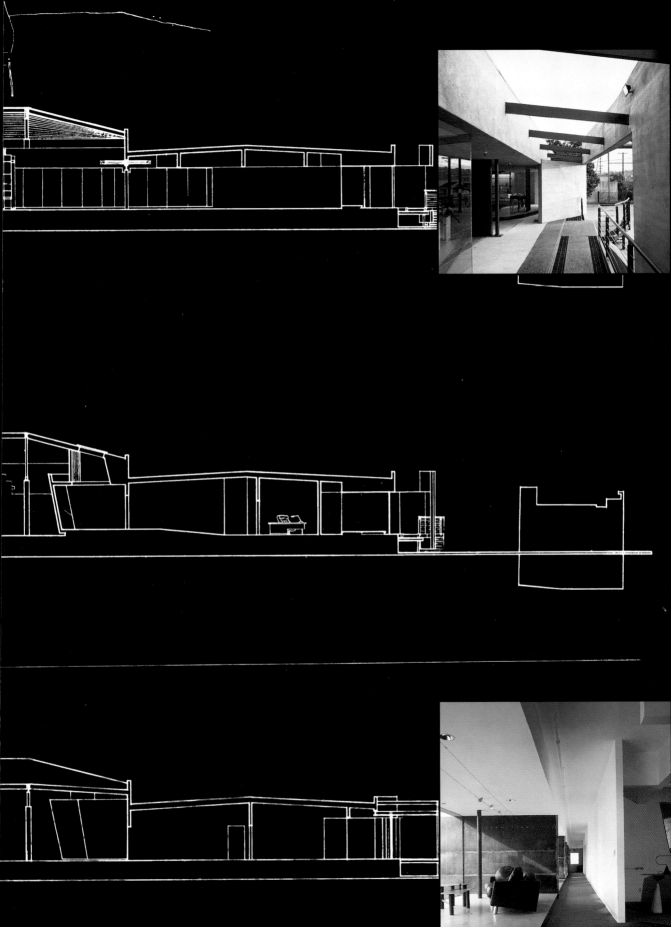

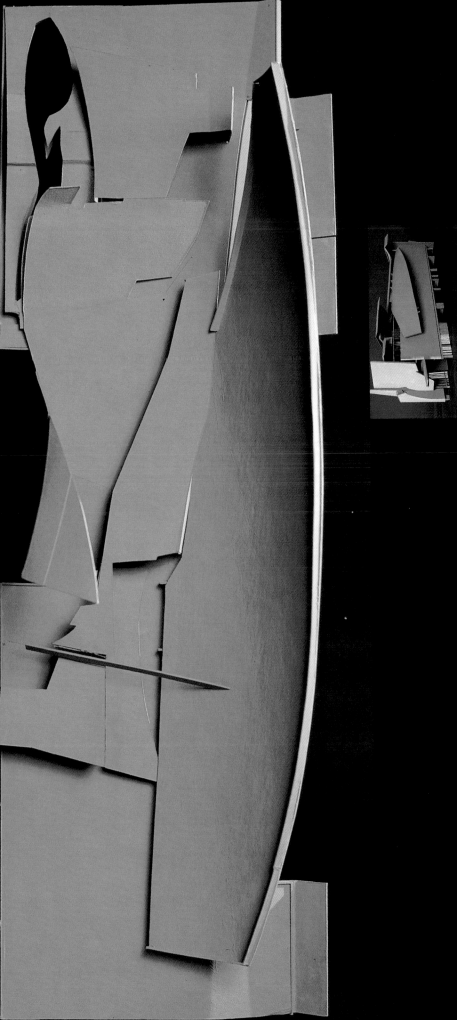

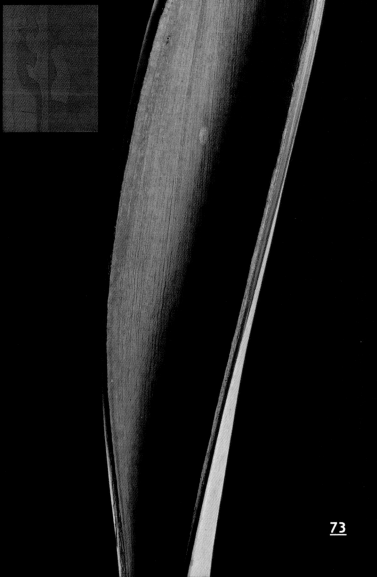

WABI involves not re-
garding incapacities as
incapacitating, not
feeling that lacking
something is depriva-
tion, not thinking that
what is not provided is
deficiency. To regard
incapacity as incapaci-
tating, to feel that
lack is deprivation, or
to believe that not be-
ing provided for is pov-
erty is not WABI but
rather the spirit of the
pauper.
—Zen-cha Roku

Meivsahna House is a container, a
vessel, in the sense that the
project strives to embody the idea
of the vessel. There is no waste,
nothing that conflicts with the
functions of protection, storage,
and retrieval. What is contained
is influenced by the shape of the
vessel and by its ability to contain,
but that is all. The vessel does not
strive to alter the thing it holds
but only to maintain its existence.

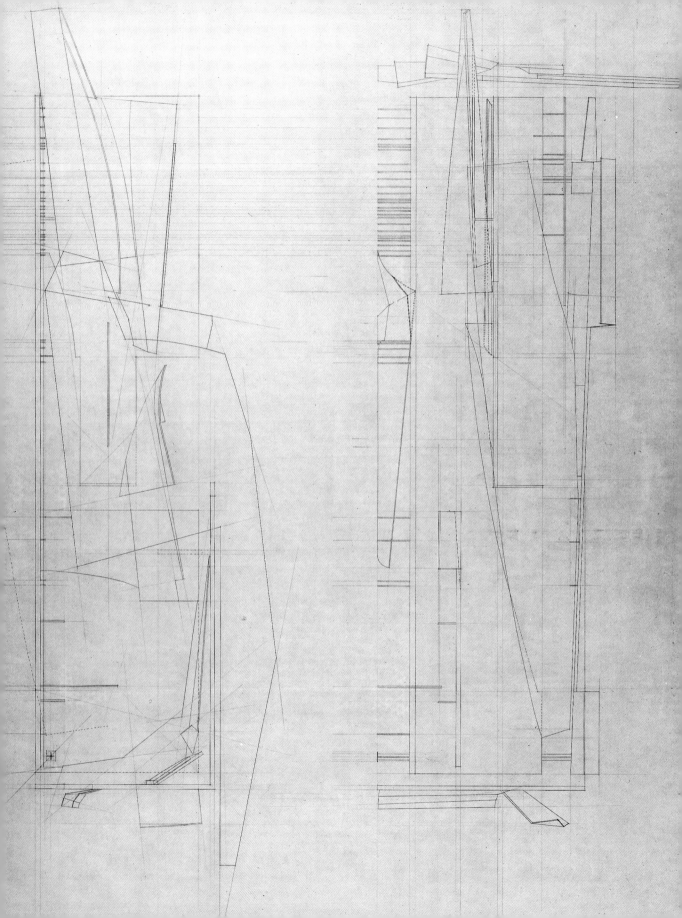

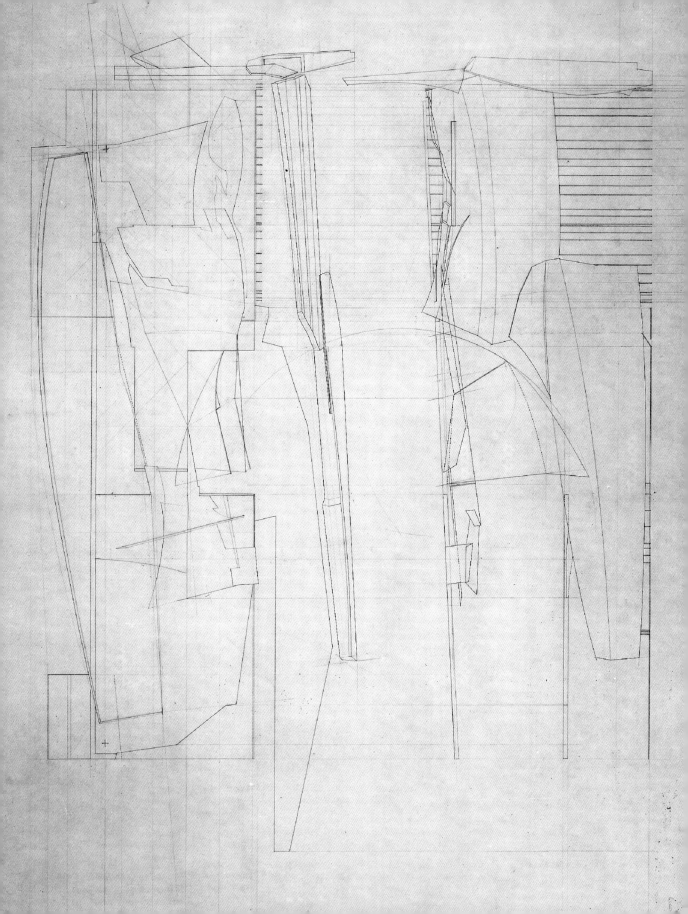

The site is a typical 50-by-150-foot flat, bookshelf lot in a neighborhood of mainly two-story houses. Meivsahna House must be viewed as a vessel that has fallen on its side; the "mouth" of this house container faces the street. Yet here lies the sense of WABI. On its side a vessel is partially useless in the typical sense, but WABI allows us to look beyond this uselessness to find what can still be used. For the house, strong vertical elements added to the sides of the mouth create the garage. The vertical pieces stabilize the vessel and give the impression of a righted object.

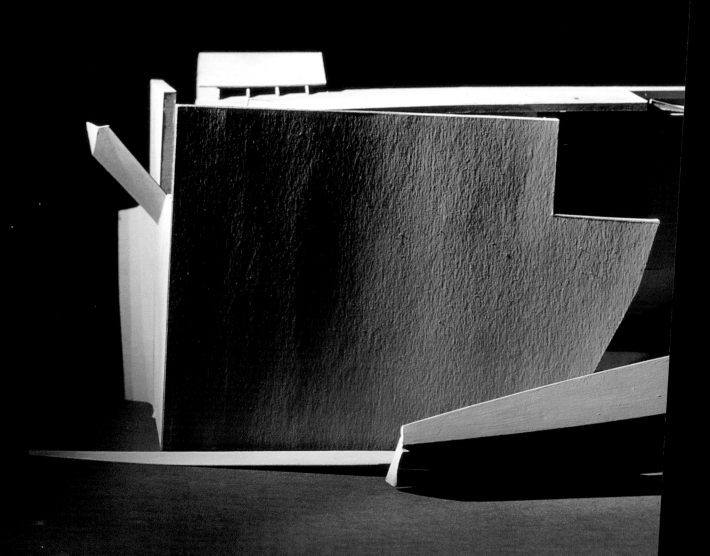

This project challenges the conventions of elemental structures, a challenge that was continued in the Golzari Guest House (see p. 144). The design is an experiment in using the distinctly separate elements of the space to achieve a sense of unity outside the ceiling, walls, and floor plan. The boxes that normally define rooms are absent in this house; rather, a change in materials, a sloped floor, and varying ceiling heights mark the passage from one "room" to another. The house is nearly a two-story loft space. From the garage, one passes through a small open courtyard and up an inclined ramp to a large studio space on the second floor where everyday activities take place. Sleeping and socializing areas are at the rear of the house, while the cooking and dining area is toward the street and lit by a flower-shaped skylight.

The structure's skin not only defines the house itself but also the outside and inside. The skin is broken in half along a single line, then the two halves are pulled apart, preserving the integrity of that line and producing the courtyard below.

[

Steel I-Beam Chair +
Alberti's Shadow Coffee Table

]

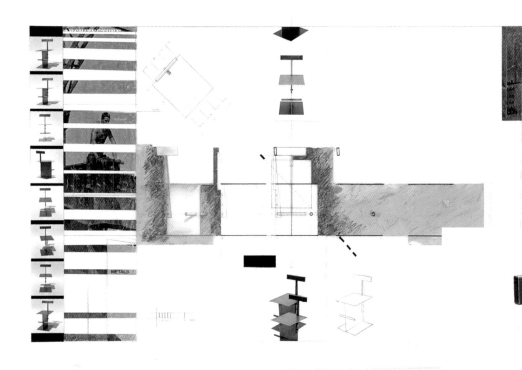

Inspired by a photograph in *Progressive Architecture* of a steelworker straddling an I-beam, this all-steel chair uses a mass-produced, I-beam-shaped element as its core component and introduces attachments to that element to provoke the user into trusting the function of the chair. A pipe footrest is welded to the central element, and a tubular steel backrest is bolted to it.

The idea for this coffee table was generated by an image of an Alberti building in which a shadow of unknown origin falls on a series of steps, producing the illusion of a three-dimensional figure within/on the stairs. The table base is a steel zigzag element, rusted and pierced with a square steel bar nested in precision-cut square holes. A sheet of glass makes minimal contact with the base and appears almost as a viewing plane.

[

Piazzale Roma Competition

1990

VENICE BIENNALE, VENICE, ITALY

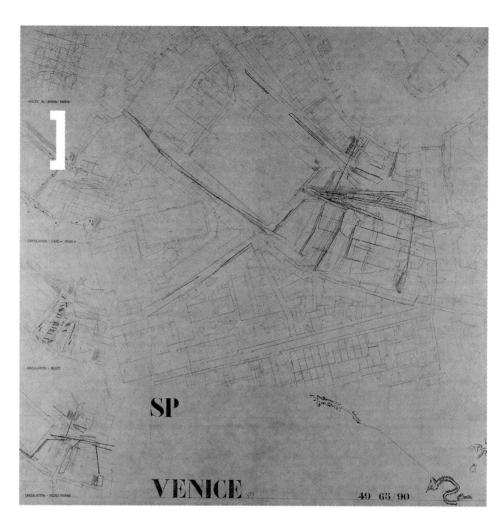

Piazzale Roma is where all that is alien to the tradition of Venice converges: the parking garage, the causeway, and the bus terminal. At present these elements are uncomfortably situated, at odds with the delicate scale of Venice and oozing pollution and confusion. Our aim is to make a new public space for these functional elements that contributes to an exploration of ancient and contemporary Venice. We created a new bridge that echoes the many small arches of Venice, a bridge that lifts you above the city to view its forms, a bridge that incorporates traditional Murano glass yet is modern.

When approached along the Via Libertà, the steel truss bridge becomes an arrow pointing into the city. Seen from the train station across the Grand Canal, the bridge appears as a facade of cantilevered glass sections growing out of the older brick and stone buildings around it, mirroring and memorializing the arch of the water in the foreground. Piers support trusses and floors at varying heights and provide access to users and services. The structure is covered with glass planes designed in cooperation with the glassblowers of Murano to represent the continuity of the craft tradition in Venice. Conceptually, the bridge can be understood as a triumphal arch inhabited by the living legions marching around its entablature. It is also a directional object.

Beyond these visual and conceptual aspects, the bridge will have two practical functions. The first is to provide a gathering place for those arriving or departing by bus, car, or taxi that facilitates one's orientation to the city. Visible from this elevated place is the Grand Canal with its vaporetto station and several other landmarks. Ramps lead from a platform down to the Grand Canal, public restrooms, a cafe, and the area near the Ponte Papadopoli, where the baggage claim and related office are located. Second, the bridge is an exhibition and orientation space where visitors can learn about Venice as it spreads out before them.

The project accommodates a compact and more logical bus depot while tripling the park area around the piazzale. On arrival at the piazzale, buses, tourist buses, cars, and taxis are immediately separated. The terminal's circulation was designed following a comparative study of bus depots to ensure the most efficient organization of traffic and to create a compact, sheltered, yet spacious passenger waiting area adjacent to the bridge. The roofs of the platforms are curved concrete forms covered with earth. The sides of the bus depot are earthen berms built to the height of those roofs. Thus, the area where buses circulate has been subsumed by newly created land. This open, undulating landscape is carefully sloped to provide access and drainage to all sides.

The park is divided through a series of low stone walls of uniform height that emerge from and disappear into the undulating earth. These walls mark the grid proposed by Le Corbusier in his Venice Hospital project, thereby casting in traditional, tactile material the modern dreams for transforming the city.

We can no longer pretend that we can create the unified civic space exemplified by the Piazza San Marco. Rather than bemoaning this fact or creating facsimiles, we propose a piazza that will be used, a fragmented gesture toward modern communal space that belongs to no person or single function. Out of the scars of modernization, the grooves of the buses, the hulk of the parking garage, the gaping holes in the urban fabric, we created a bridge of faith.

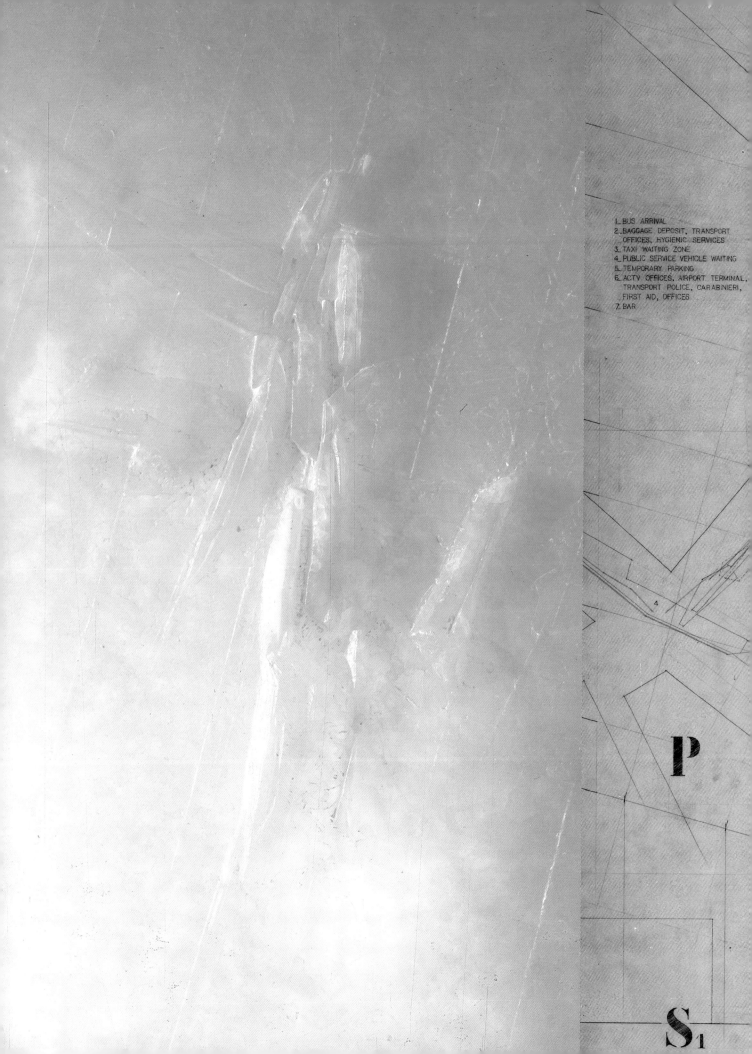

1. BUS ARRIVAL
2. BAGGAGE DEPOSIT, TRANSPORT
   OFFICES, HYGIENIC SERVICES
3. TAXI WAITING ZONE
4. PUBLIC SERVICE VEHICLE WAITING
5. TEMPORARY PARKING
6. ACTV OFFICES, AIRPORT TERMINAL,
   TRANSPORT POLICE, CARABINIERI,
   FIRST AID, OFFICES
7. BAR

4

P

S₁

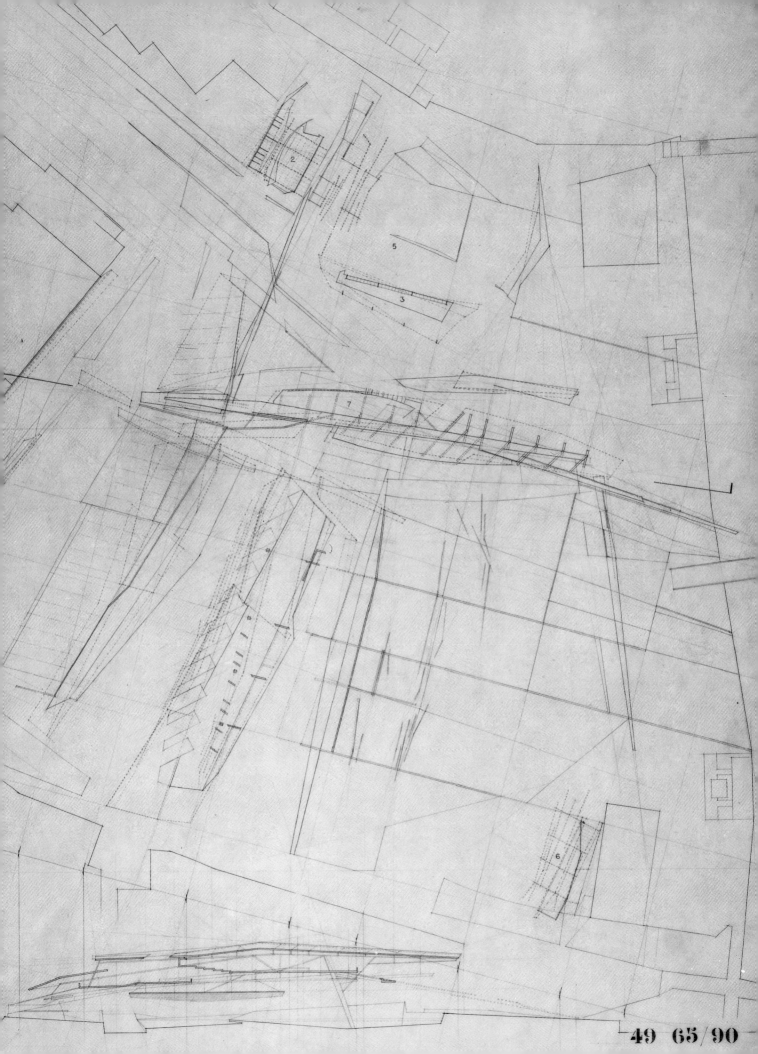

49 65/90

[

sun House]

FULLERTON

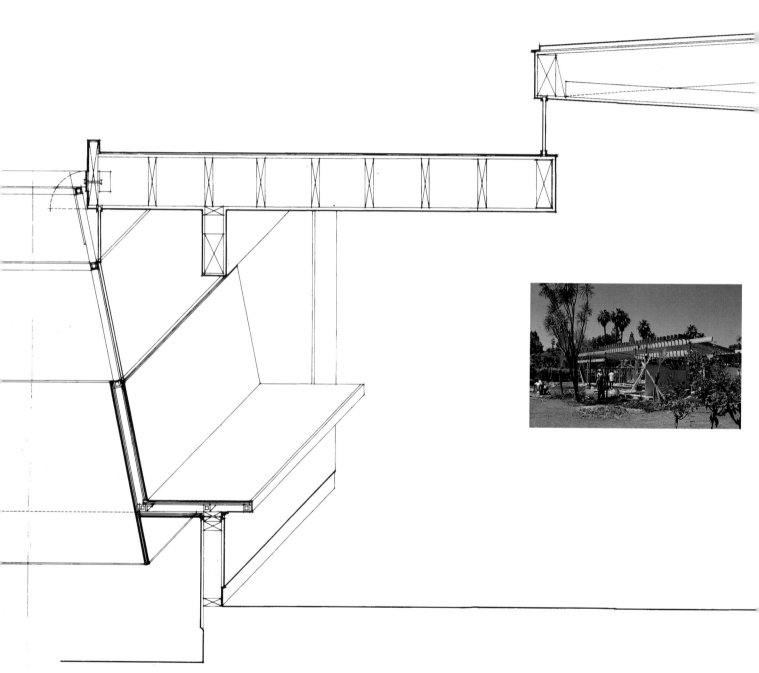

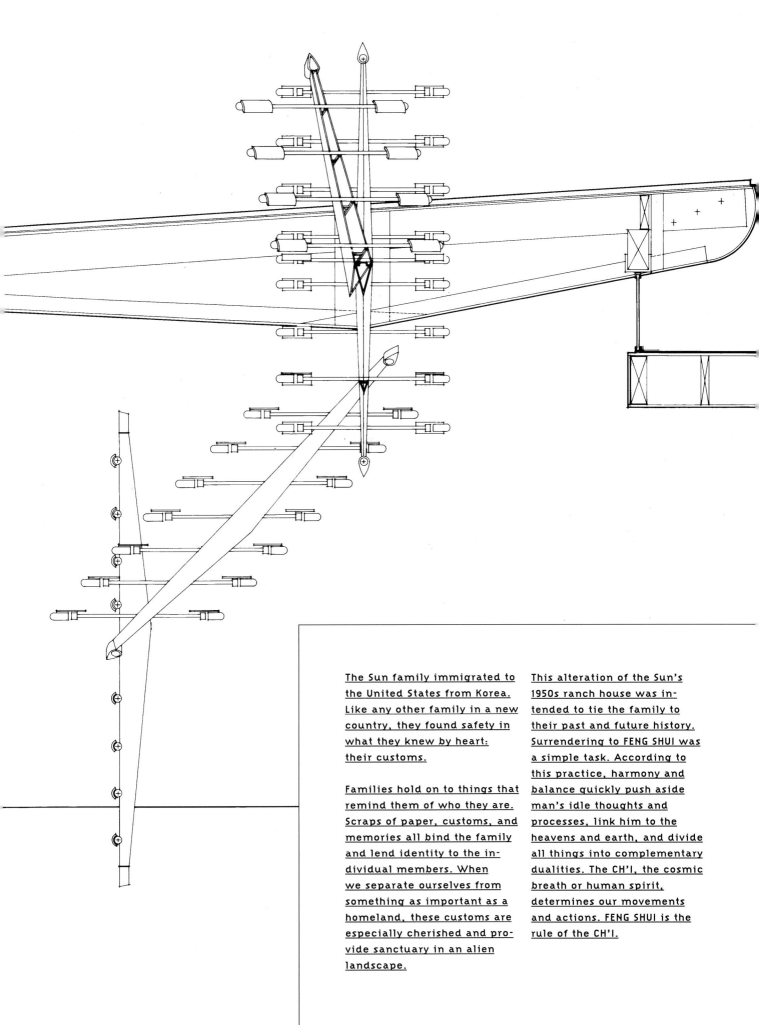

The Sun family immigrated to the United States from Korea. Like any other family in a new country, they found safety in what they knew by heart: their customs.

Families hold on to things that remind them of who they are. Scraps of paper, customs, and memories all bind the family and lend identity to the individual members. When we separate ourselves from something as important as a homeland, these customs are especially cherished and provide sanctuary in an alien landscape.

This alteration of the Sun's 1950s ranch house was intended to tie the family to their past and future history. Surrendering to FENG SHUI was a simple task. According to this practice, harmony and balance quickly push aside man's idle thoughts and processes, link him to the heavens and earth, and divide all things into complementary dualities. The CH'I, the cosmic breath or human spirit, determines our movements and actions. FENG SHUI is the rule of the CH'I.

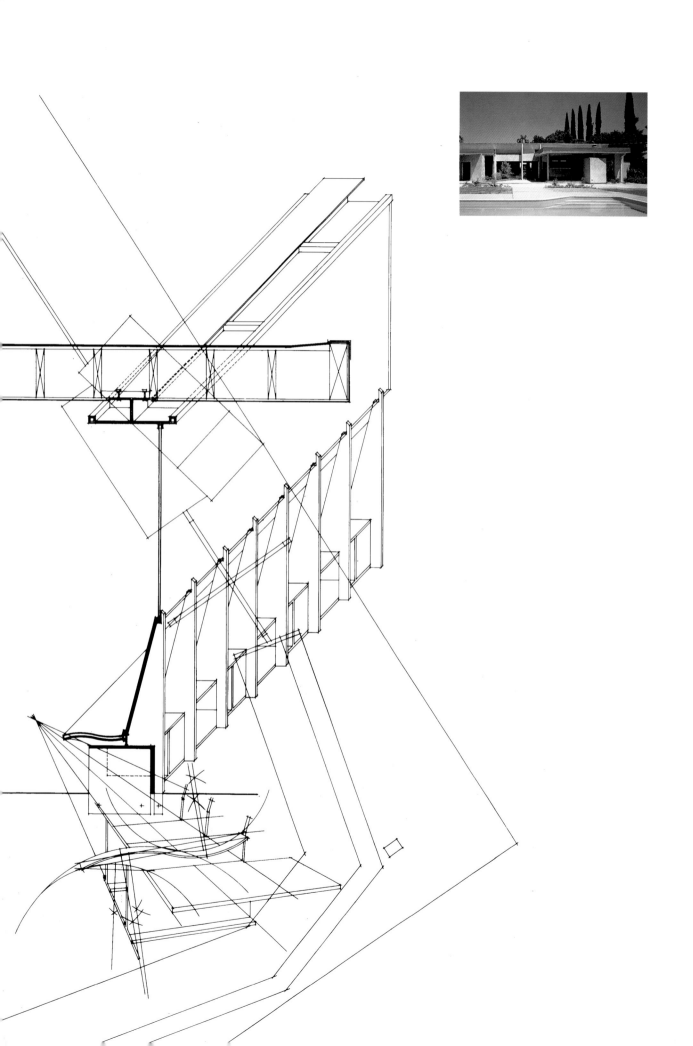

[H e a v e n + EARTH   ]

The design divided the house into
TWO PARTS symbolizing heaven and earth:

THE ROOF,
which is separate from the body of the house
beneath;

THE GROUND
formed in response to the needs of the structure
and the roof.

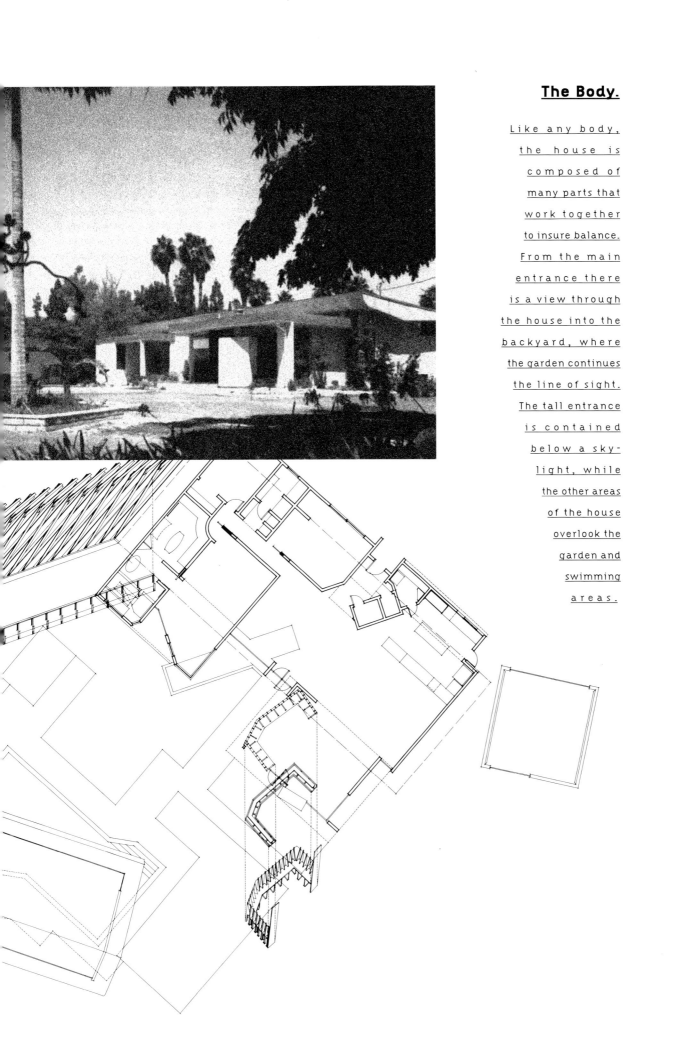

The Body.

Like any body, the house is composed of many parts that work together to insure balance. From the main entrance there is a view through the house into the backyard, where the garden continues the line of sight. The tall entrance is contained below a sky-light, while the other areas of the house overlook the garden and swimming areas.

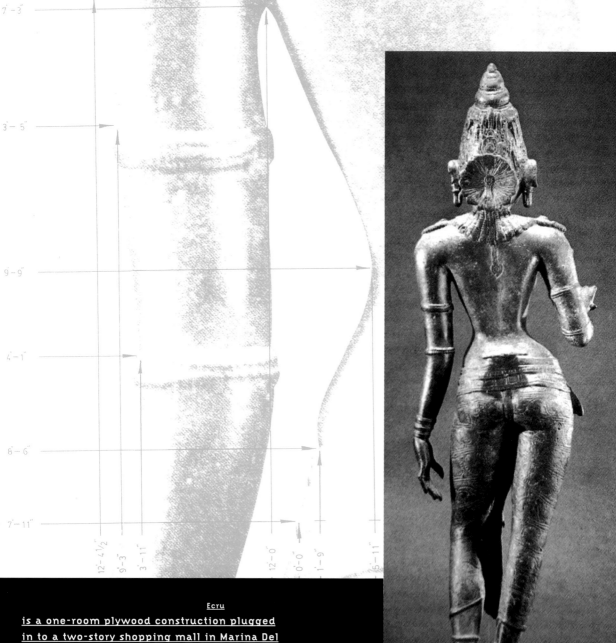

Ecru
is a one-room plywood construction plugged
in to a two-story shopping mall in Marina Del
Rey. Angeli Mare (see p. 104) is also located
here, and both projects treat the mall as a
vessel. A protruding glass display case breaks
up the typical blank mall storefront and is
supported by a glass wall that slices into the
facade. A portion of the first Ecru store's
typeface facade (see p. 58) was enlarged and
applied here to tie the new store to the
original one on Melrose Avenue.

Clothing is closer to our body than any other designed object, so the human body became the obvious inspiration for the project. The design began with a fortuitous experiment that resulted when the line drawings presented to the carpenter did not accurately represent the desired construction shapes and a template was required. The sections, elevations, and storefront figure were abstracted from the seductive shapes of a sculpted Indian figurine and rendered as cardboard templates. Carpenters used these to build frames of 3/4 inch plywood sheathed with 1/4 inch plywood. The sheets initially would not bend to the shapes defined by the templates and had to be scored on the back to prevent the plywood from breaking. Through experimentation, one successful panel was eventually produced and became the pattern for the rest. Disassociated from the specific representation of flesh, the plywood suggested the idea of skin's smooth, uniform attractiveness.

The idea of the template is important in many of these projects and was crucial to the concept of the Ecru store in Marina del Rey. There is truth in a template: It momentarily removes the responsibility for the process from the maker, puts to rest fears of error, and reinforces our desire for an object. For this project, the templates were constructed on the floor of the studio, with knees to the concrete, palms on corrugated cardboard, the sound of metal slicing and ripping the corrugation. We ran our fingers along the freshly cut lines, stood the templates up, and stood back, approving and disapproving. We looked through one template at another, referencing the drawings, the photos, the proportional system that stemmed from the figurine template. The work was fueled by the desire to be lost in the process of making. The templates became objects that encapsulated the notion of working in the present, of no visual beginning or end.

Because the surrounding context is a marina, the art of shipbuilding became a source of form. The ceiling of the store is shaped like the bottom of a boat and was constructed of scored drywall panels. A cantilevered sales counter and eight-foot-tall pivoting mirrors are the focus of the interior. Lighting is installed in eye-shaped recesses in the walls and in ribs along the ceiling. A single, steel-bar handle for the pivoting glass door is accessible on the inside and outside.

The sensuous curves of the walls and the well-defined shape of the figurine in the column and facade reveal the importance of layers. Ecru celebrates "the depiction of the body as a living garment," as described in Vol. 2 of ZONE: FRAGMENTS FOR A HISTORY OF THE HUMAN BODY. It equates layers of skin with layers of clothing and forces the observer to look for the hidden, for the secret. Peeking behind the walls is akin to the erotic play of skirt on thigh; to exposing too much arm, chest, calf; to the seductive glimpse of a belly.

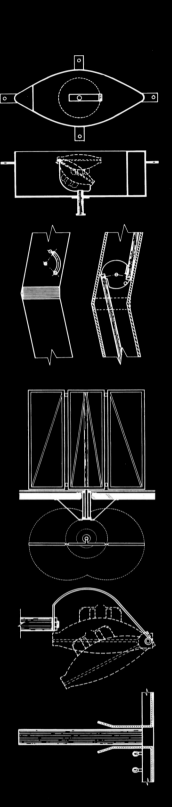

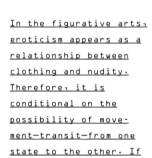

In the figurative arts, eroticism appears as a relationship between clothing and nudity. Therefore, it is conditional on the possibility of movement—transit—from one state to the other. If

either of these poles takes on a primary or essential significance to the exclusion of the other, then the possibility for this transit is sacrificed, and with it the conditions for eroticism. In such cases, either clothing or nudity becomes an absolute value.

—Mario Perniola,
"Between Clothing and Nudity," in
ZONE: Fragments for a History of the Human Body,
Vol. 2 (1989)

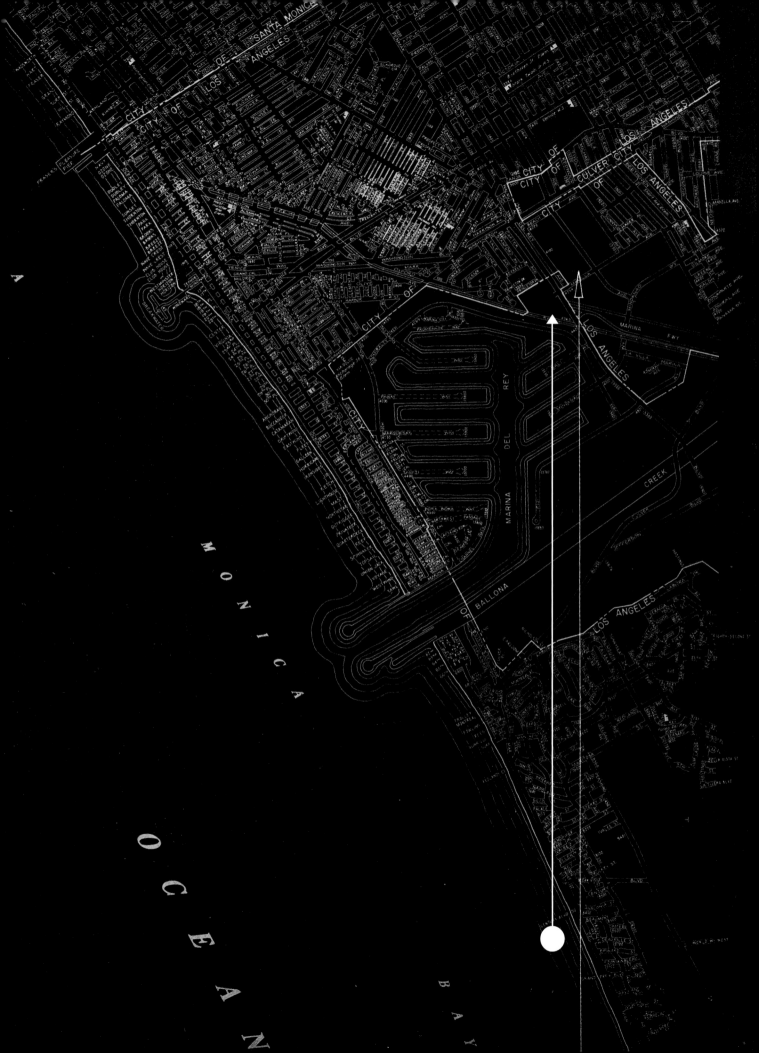

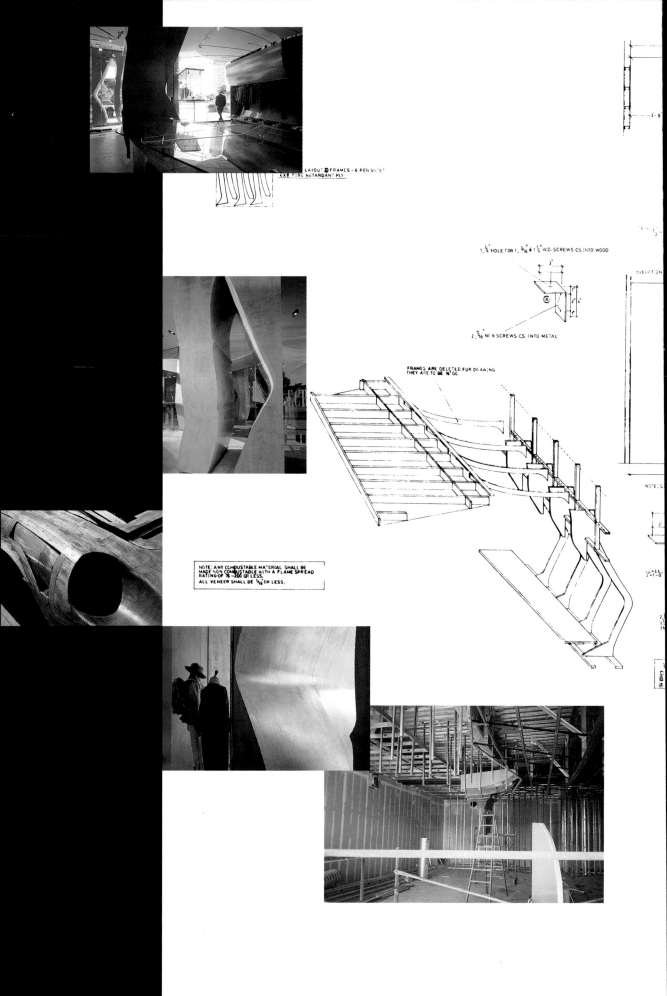

LAYOUT ⑧ FRAMES - 6 PER SHEET
4 X 8 FIRE RETARDANT PLY

1, 1/2" HOLE FOR 1, 3/16" ⌀ 1 1/2" W.D. SCREWS CS. INTO WOOD

Ⓐ

2, 7/16" NO. 6 SCREWS CS. INTO METAL

FRAMES ARE DELETED FOR DRAWING
THEY ARE TO BE 16" O.C.

NOTE: ANY COMBUSTABLE MATERIAL SHALL BE
MADE NON COMBUSTABLE WITH A FLAME SPREAD
RATING OF 76 -200 OR LESS.
ALL VENEER SHALL BE 1/16 OR LESS.

104

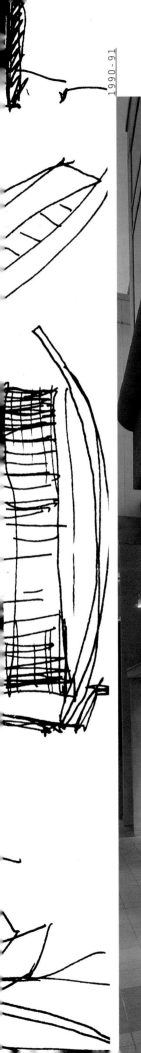

[Angeli Mare]

The design for Angeli Mare responds to the concept of the plug-in building, a new structure inserted within an existing one, and to the context of the Venice marina. The craft of shipbuilding inspired the choice of materials, form, and structure. The restaurant is in an oversized mini-mall, one of many developed in Southern California during the 1980s.

This uninspiring host building provided all of the essentials: 4,000 square feet of space, parking, water, gas, trash room, and security guards. The first intent was to distinguish the restaurant from the mall, to develop a new ordering system that contradicted the existing building.

On the exterior, the facade of steel, glass, and polished, stained plywood makes the restaurant appear completely detached from the existing building, as if the mall were built around it or the restaurant had been moved to this location and slipped underneath the mall. The massing of the building expresses the project's specific programmatic needs. The structure is broken into four distinct yet interconnected parts: entrance, bar, dining area, and kitchen area, housed in a space 33 feet wide by 120 feet long and 14 feet high.

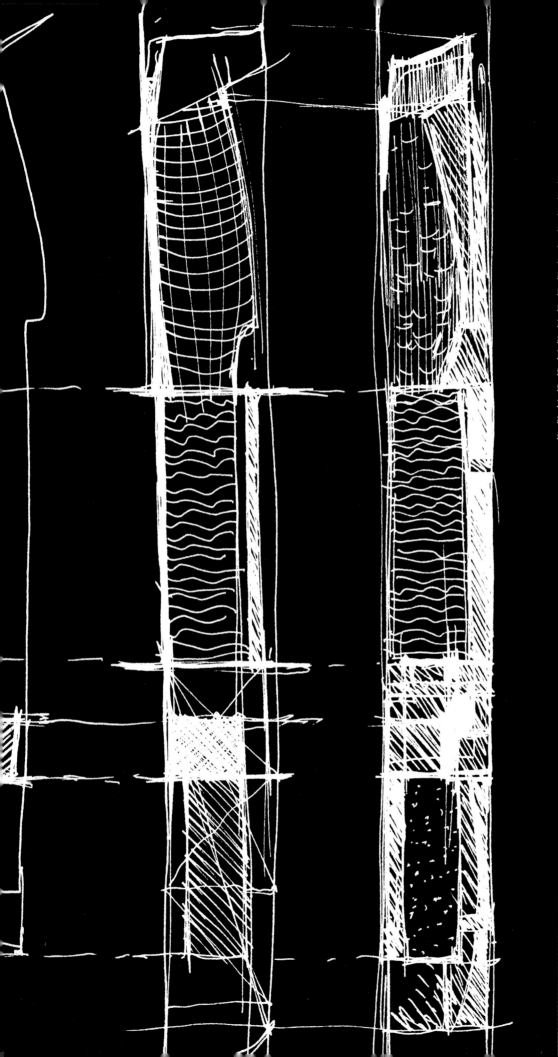

One might assume that Southern California's climate would ensure an abundance of outdoor dining facilities, but this is not so. In this case, the unattractive, strip-mall site and strict building codes prevented entertaining even the idea of eating outside. My nostalgic response was to bring outdoor space in by constructing a large, trellis-like ribbed ceiling that recalls outdoor dining places in Tuscany. At the same time, the design speaks of ship construction and the ribs of fish or humans.

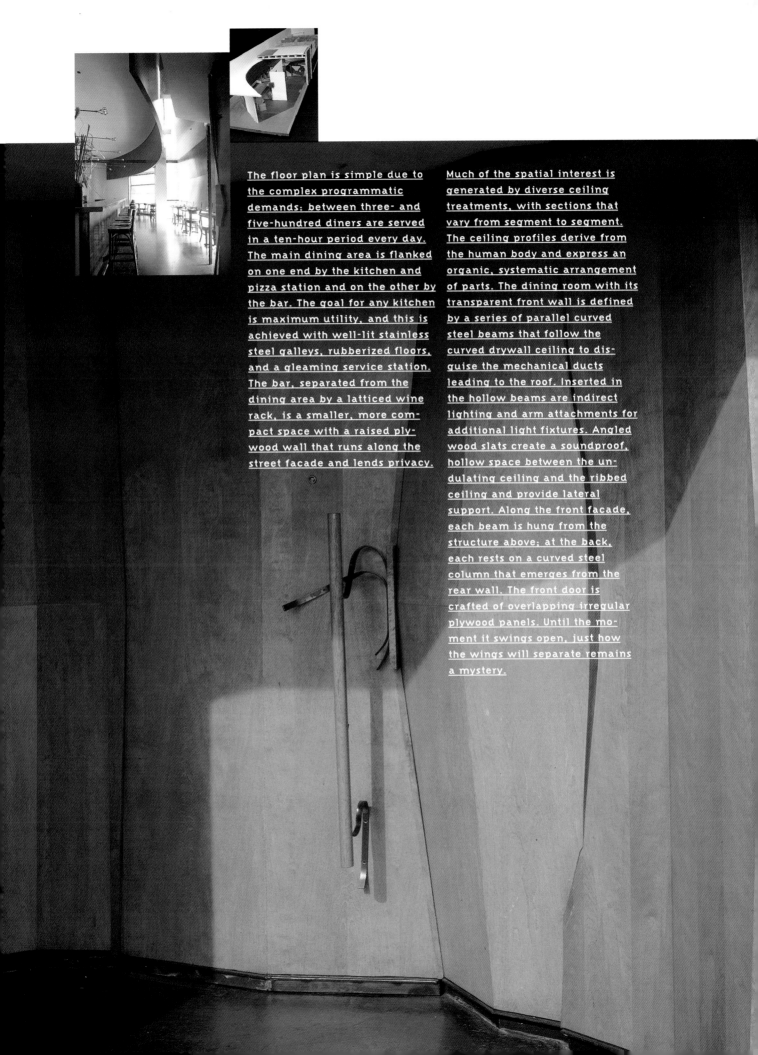

The floor plan is simple due to the complex programmatic demands: between three- and five-hundred diners are served in a ten-hour period every day. The main dining area is flanked on one end by the kitchen and pizza station and on the other by the bar. The goal for any kitchen is maximum utility, and this is achieved with well-lit stainless steel galleys, rubberized floors, and a gleaming service station. The bar, separated from the dining area by a latticed wine rack, is a smaller, more compact space with a raised plywood wall that runs along the street facade and lends privacy.

Much of the spatial interest is generated by diverse ceiling treatments, with sections that vary from segment to segment. The ceiling profiles derive from the human body and express an organic, systematic arrangement of parts. The dining room with its transparent front wall is defined by a series of parallel curved steel beams that follow the curved drywall ceiling to disguise the mechanical ducts leading to the roof. Inserted in the hollow beams are indirect lighting and arm attachments for additional light fixtures. Angled wood slats create a soundproof, hollow space between the undulating ceiling and the ribbed ceiling and provide lateral support. Along the front facade, each beam is hung from the structure above; at the back, each rests on a curved steel column that emerges from the rear wall. The front door is crafted of overlapping irregular plywood panels. Until the moment it swings open, just how the wings will separate remains a mystery.

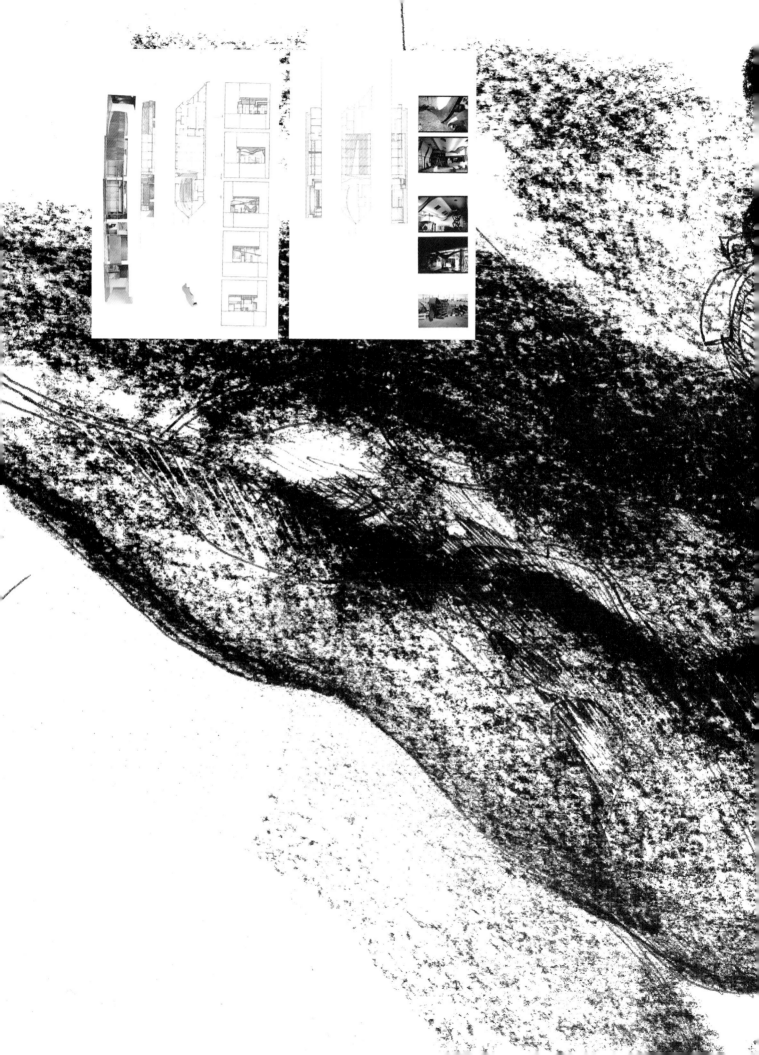

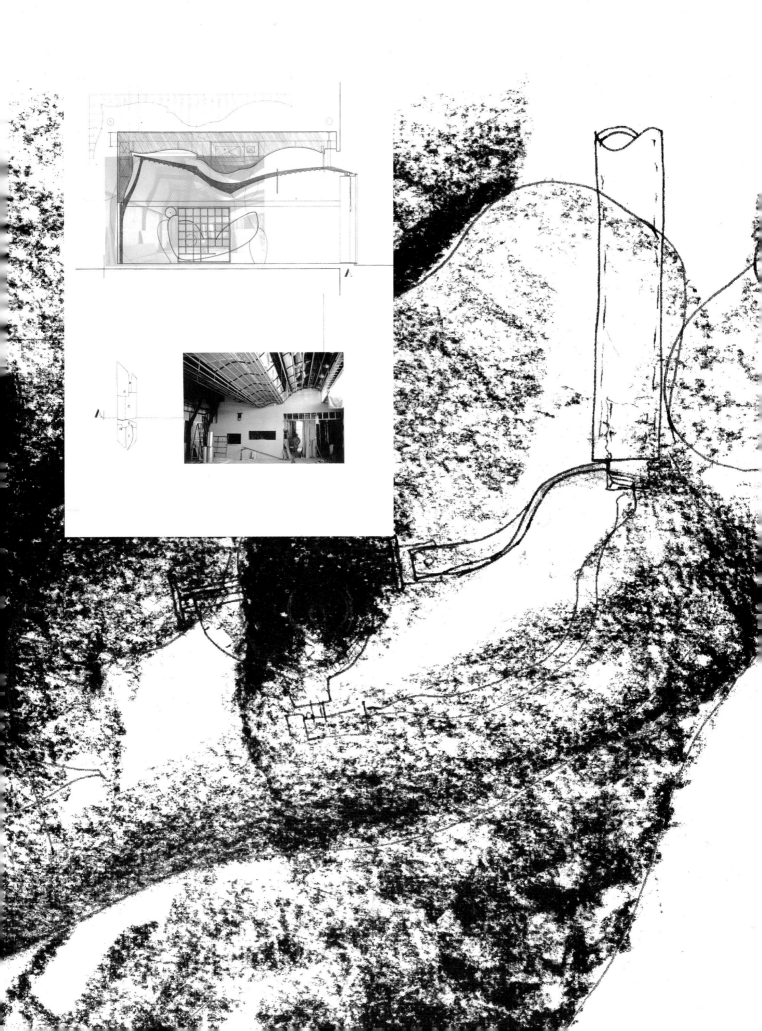

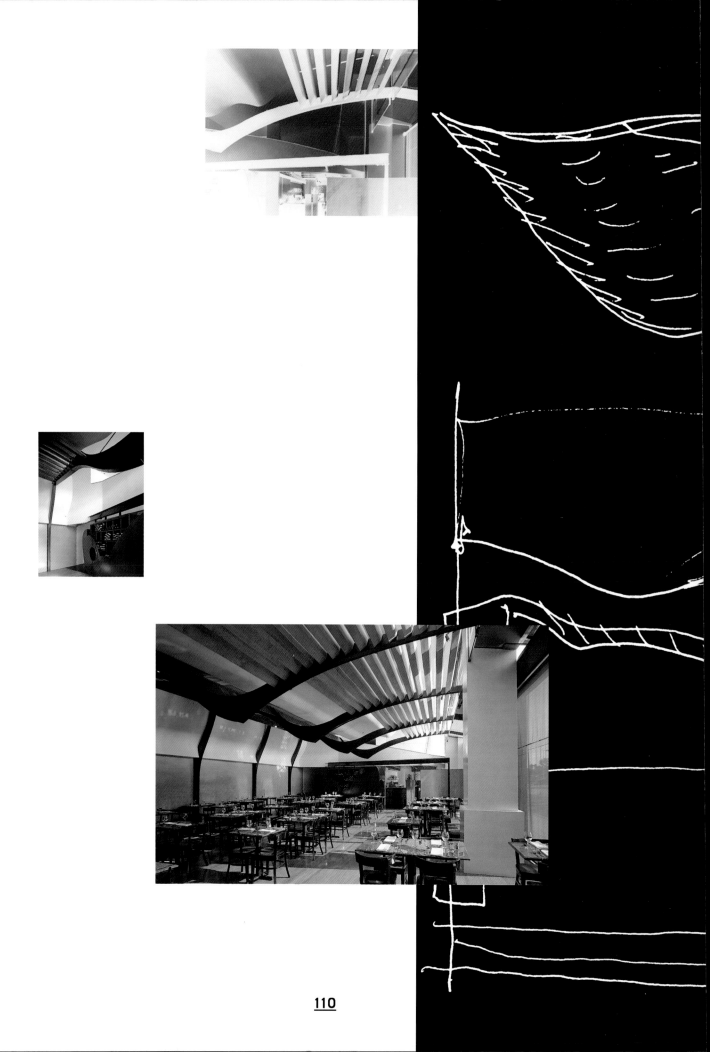

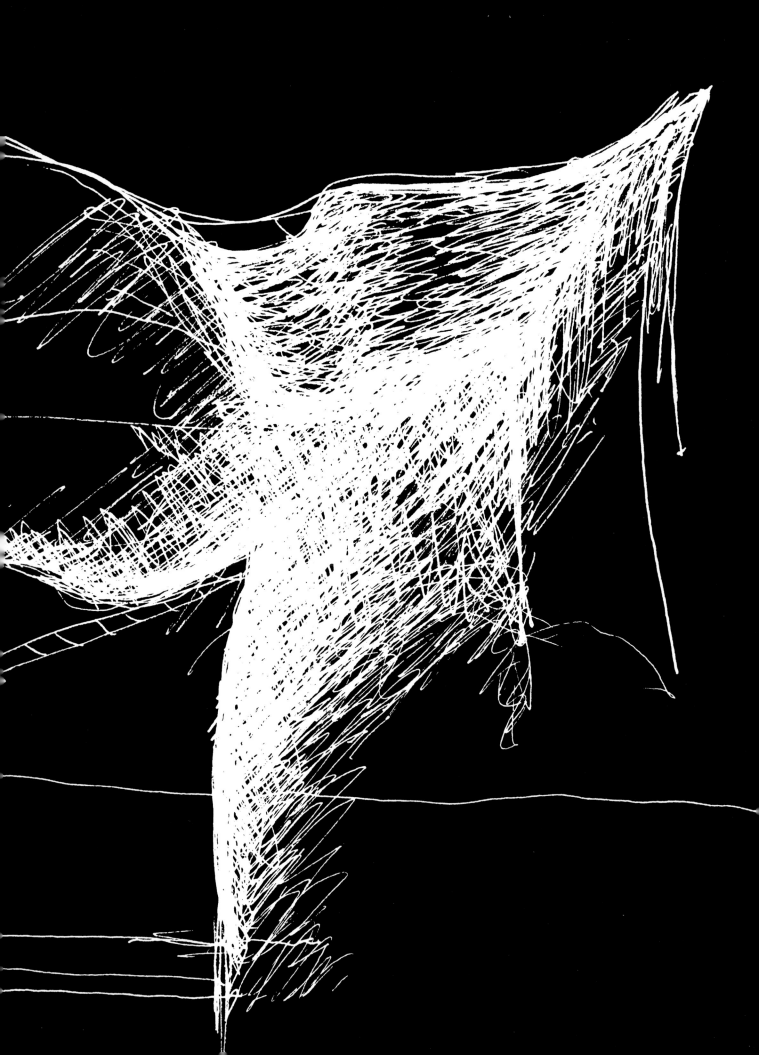

This store primarily consists of one room and is a simple, almost reserved project in relationship to others built at this time. Display cases run along each side of the store in front of two gently curved plywood walls. Arching light fixtures along the top of the walls light the cases directly opposite and form a delicate ribbed canopy. The shorter cases are supported by a steel frame, while the taller cases are elevated from their plywood bases on glass planes that lend them a light, almost hovering quality.

This is also a project about reuse. The opportunity to design Pave came up around the same time that the Ecru Melrose store went out of business. We reasoned that Ecru's plywood components and display cases could be reused on the Pave project rather than destroyed or sold. The recession in Los Angeles in the late 1980s had radically changed the building economy and produced an economic climate very receptive to reuse.

Built for a specific context, the Ecru pieces at first seemed static, to speak a language that did not wish to be translated or applied to another structure. But in fact, slightly altering the pieces generated a space with a true historical, but not a direct visual, connection to Ecru. Both projects involved retail and the passion for layering the body. The adjustments were not radical but altogether logical for the new store: display cases were raised, walls trimmed, lighting altered.

This project dispels some of the reuse myths, because form derived from a single context buries itself in that context alone. In Pave we also see many of the elements that were used in other projects such as Angeli Mare, the Ecru store in Marina del Rey, and Capitaine Restaurant.

[

Pave

Brentwood

Jewelry

Store]

Once an architect has a T-square in his hand,
he can no longer think architecture.

He can only think about drawing it.

—**Bruno Zevi**, The Modern Language of Architecture

Hides

by Michele Saee

This sketchbook filled with drawings I made in Paris a few years ago expresses what I feel about something so fundamental to architecture that we take it for granted—drawing itself. I am always thinking through and about architecture, dissecting the methods and processes we use to create architecture and drawing and writing these notions in my sketchbooks. Yet I felt that on its own this type of examination was limited, as if it could only tell me what is already known and show me what is already seen. I wanted also to draw as if for the first time, to be caught up in the thrill of discoveries that were genuinely new to me; to keep moving back and forth, randomly and unpredictably, between forays into unmapped territories and reflections on the wisdom we derive from other times and cultures. This book marks the beginning of this process.

It is not easy to describe the value of drawing in the development of thought, since this process is different for each of us. "Drawing," said Joseph Beuys, in a statement that I find very moving, "is the first visible form in my work, the first visible thing of the form of the thought, the changing point from the invisible powers to the visible thing."

The sketches reproduced here are not commonly considered architectural drawings. They do not represent buildings or show how they might be built. They are not studies of the urban environment and do not describe the forms that can spark inspiration for a building. But for me these very personal drawings are architectural, and they describe how I see the world before I express this seeing as a conscious thought or a piece of writing or a building. Drawing as a way of communicating what we know about our world is as old as cave paintings and as new as the computer-assisted images sent from satellites spinning toward the outer reaches of the universe.

The ability to draw as a way of expressing what we see is innate in the human species. Children begin to draw and then to tell stories through their drawings, making their inner worlds visible to others. They do so until they become self-conscious, concerned about expressing the same reality that those around them claim to see. The ability to describe visually the worlds that they imagine so vividly begins to dim and they start to think of their drawings as "wrong" rather than as merely images that adults have lost the power to see.

From the time of Newton until Einstein announced his theory of relativity, the accepted metaphor for our universe was something solid and ordered, a big machine that might be planned and built in a way similar to architecture as it is traditionally conceived. In the twentieth century the focus of physics has shifted from the material properties of our universe to the mathematical laws that describe its behavior. The metaphor is now a big thought rather than a big machine, and the design process and our perception of context have shifted accordingly. The process of creating space used to be informed only by what was physically proximate, but with new communications networks the entire globe is now close by. Earlier means of evaluating, analyzing, and documenting the design process are now limited in nature and scale; today we inhabit space measured physically, against our bodies, and mentally, according to the power, speed, and scope of our technologies.

Life and architecture are inextricably bound together. A life rich in simple things, in family, in striving for kindness and completeness, and in an appreciation of mystery and beauty, absolutely includes architecture. In addressing life through architecture and architecture through life we can avoid the artificial and deadening qualities that can arise in architecture that addresses only itself. My work is driven by the belief that the process of making is the most important part of architecture and that in making things we also become aware of the changeable nature of the world around us—from the cycles of the seasons, with plants germinating, maturing, and dying, to the similar birth and death of ideas.

The story of urban life is through bodily experience. It is a story of the deepest parts of life—how women and men moved in public and private spaces, what they saw and heard, the smells that assailed their noses, where they ate, how they dressed, the mores of bathing and making love all in the spaces of the city. The contemporary problem is the sensory deprivation which seems to curse most modern building, the dullness, the monotony, and the tactile sterility which afflicts the urban environment.

—Richard Sennett, Flesh and Stone

All of our senses are active, but the lion's share of our perceptions is weighted toward the visual. Architecture is about the experience of the human body in space, and using all of our senses in the making of architectural space is critical. We must go beyond perceiving space as something we merely see and creating architecture only from lines we lay down on a page, evaluated principally by how pleasing they might be to the eye.

"We really studied," Miles Davis once said of his artistic process. "If a door squeaked, we would call out the exact pitch. And every time I heard the chord of G, for example, my fingers automatically took the position for C sharp on the horn the flatted fifth whether I was playing or not."

—Thomas Stearns, Story of Jazz

I wanted to draw without restrictions, without inventing limitations to impose on my work, and to stop editing my aspirations. I had to suspend both judgment and disbelief. I wanted to go beyond the self-consciousness that our culture exhibits toward technology. Instead, I wanted to be concerned with what we might do and how we might live once we got to the point where we were no longer self-conscious. I began to use a device familiar to science fiction writers—projecting forward to a time when these technologies would be taken for granted as rich and expressive part of life—so I could consider how to engage and express this richness through architecture.

Day and night he will work, making many false starts, filling the trash with unsuccessful chains of equations and logical sequences. But some evenings he will return to his desk knowing he has learned things about nature that no-one has ever known, ventured into the forest and found light, gotten hold of precious secrets. On those evenings, his heart will pound as if he were in love.

—Alan Lightman, Einstein's Dreams

[Atwater **Tea + Coffee** House

ATWATER VILLAGE

The Atwater Tea +

Coffee House

creates illusion. The distinctive curved shape of the booths that form the walls reflects sound, turning the space into a whispering chamber. Patrons' conversations bounce off the curved walls and are heard throughout the cafe. Some patrons embrace this effect, but others alter their converations as a result, questioning the role of the senses in a cafe.

Artwork hangs on the walls behind and above the seats, so people find their gaze drawn in the direction of the person sitting opposite. Eyes cannot help but flicker and meet on occasion, and patrons are eased into a partnership of shared activity: looking and talking. While Atwater Tea and Coffee House is composed of many parts, figuratively there is only one table. Unity characterizes the space.

[

proprio**ception**

FLORIDA A+M UNIVERSITY/TALLAHASSEE

]

"Proprioception"

was an installation designed and built with architecture students of Florida A&M University during a two-week workshop on the A&M campus. "Art Works for Children" was an installation constructed for the City of Los Angeles in support of a benefit for the Center for the Vulnerable Child, held at the W.B.Petitfils house designed by Paul Williams.

Both projects stepped outside the constraints of economics and power to allow the built work to be influenced not by the client's financial priorities but by poetry, history, and the grace and art that inspire the creation of space. The projects addressed freedom of expression unburdened by the weight of practicality. In some sense, however, these were practical projects. They cost little to build, defined a tangible space, and enriched the experience of those who built them.

The body knows itself.
ARCHITECTURAL EDUCATION AND PRACTICE HAVE OVEREMPHASIZED THE VISUAL ASPECT OF BUILT FORM AND HAVE NOT ENCOURAGED US TO USE OUR BODIES AS A MEDIUM FOR TRANSFORMING STRUCTURE.

The maker knows its body.
THE MAKER'S BODY IS BOUND BY ITS FORM AND RELEASED BY ITS COMPLEXITY. THE STRUCTURE OF THE BODY GUIDES ITS ABILITY TO FUNCTION AS A TOOL. WERE THE BODY ALTERED, THE TOOL WOULD PRODUCE A DIFFERENT WORK.

The body is a tool.
BOTH OF THESE PROJECTS CELEBRATED THIS IDEA AND USED THE BODY TO SHAPE THEIR COMPONENTS. THE BODY'S POSITION AND ITS RESPONSE TO THE CONSTRUCTION MATERIAL GENERATED THE FORM.

At Florida A&M, a plot of ground on campus was excavated by digging two six-foot-deep trenches, one eighty feet long and the other sixty feet long and perpendicular to the first. Observers descended into these trenches to view the body of the earth. Here in the rich, clinging, red Georgia clay were the foundations of the school, the ground bracing the buildings. Four-foot-wide sheets of galvanized metal cut from a roll were shaped to create a cover for the excavated ground, using the body as the only tool. The sheets were bent around hands and thighs to shape curves, wrapped around the back like a blanket, forced against knees to tighten the bends in the metal.

The primary concern of current building activity is financial, and so its products are mostly marketable commodities. Those who design and build as a profession engage in operations that must yield profits to their promoters, so they cannot evade the requirements of economic power and become inherently a party to making architecture a commodity.

—Giancarlo de Carlo

The Road That is Not a Road, 1993

[

Art Works
for Children]

As conceived initially, "Art Works for Children"

was to be constructed in the studio and transported to the Paul Williams house. When transporting the piece became impossible, it was built on site, in the courtyard of the house. The installation became a link to history—an opportunity to respond to Paul Williams's work, his role in Los Angeles architecture, and his accomplishments.

Here the body was used again to shape the one-inch-diameter rod that defined the piece. The rod reflected movement, a dynamic. Its curves and the intervals between bends suggested both calm and intensity, the essence of human interaction. This piece could only have been constructed manually: you could see evidence of the hand and arms in the curves, the reach of a limb in the length of the rod, and the human power of creation in its height. The two installations were similar. The shapes produced by wrapping the rod in cloth for "Art Works for Children" recalled the metal sheets bent by the Florida students; in a sense, one body informed both projects.

The body is not a static tool. It learns through process. What is successful is repeated and expanded on to further develop form. The body also changes in response to pain—in the case of these projects, the cuts and sore muscles and hands caused by using the body in new ways. These physiological alterations affected the physical form of the projects: trying to bend metal without further injuring one's finger, for example, produced shapes that were different from those anticipated. These subtle changes reflected the idea that our form predefines what we can make.

The working process used in these installations questioned the principal issues that architects are concerned with and attempted to demonstrate that the way we produce architecture today is perverse. We produce *for* the body, not *with* body, as if physicality were some distant concept that could only be grasped abstractly. The quality of architectural models, the heights of walls, the bends in steel all reflect the body's capacity to function as a tool. As makers and thinkers we aim to produce a better quality of life; yet in our work the body *is* life. Only by using the body to generate the work can the work itself celebrate the body.

proprio**ception**

the vital "sixth sense" by which **the body** knows itself and judges with perfect, instantaneous, automatic **precision** all its movable parts, their **relationship** to one another,

and their alignment

in space

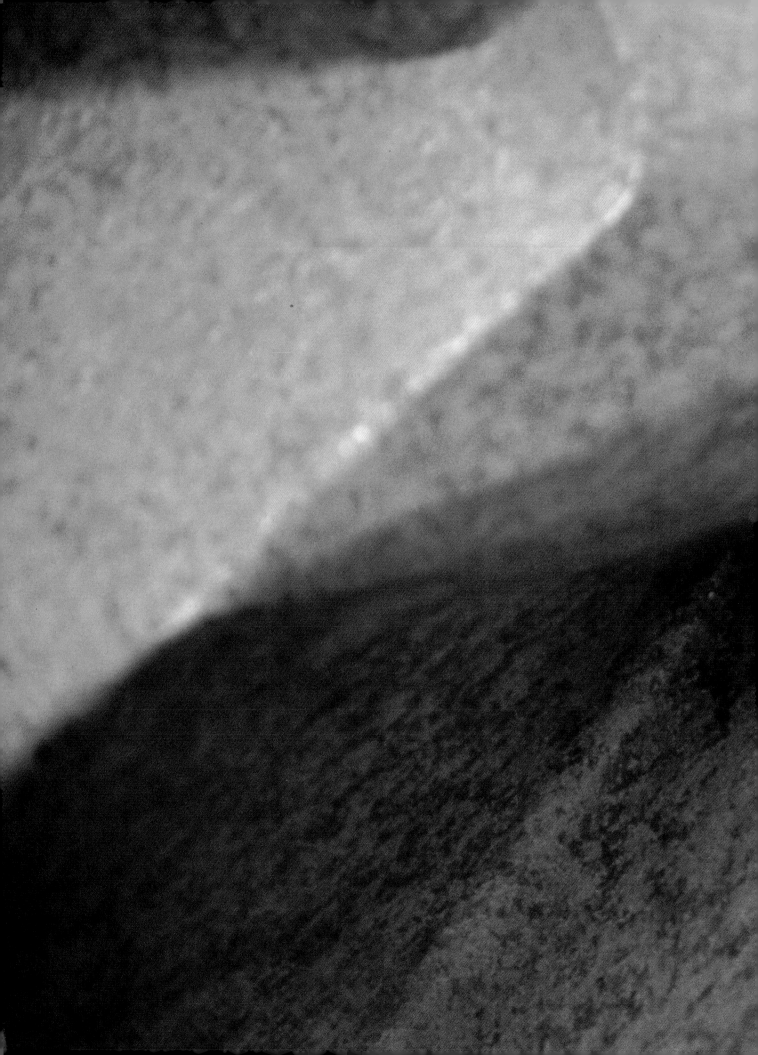

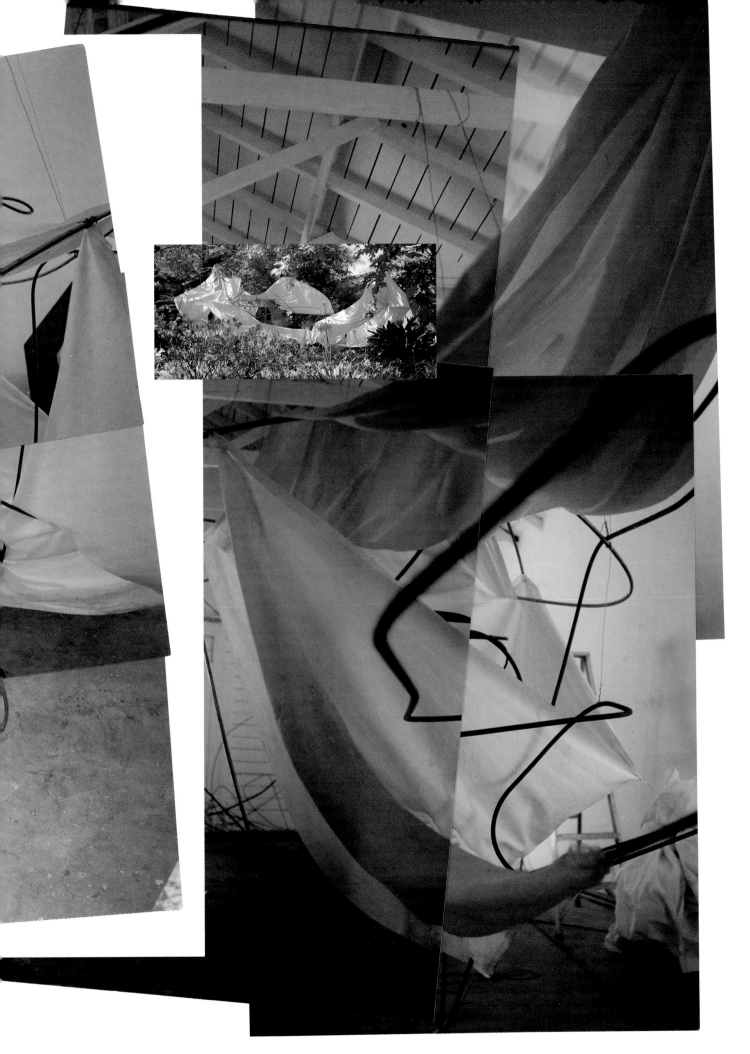

BEVERLY HILLS

[Beverly Hills
Cosmetic **Dental**
Clinic
]

Trips to the dentist are associated with particular feelings and ideas engendered by contact with one's culture and by personal experience. Standard dental office architecture reinforces these feelings, producing a sense of isolation through unattractive, plain spaces that do not allow the patient any activity except the perusal of waiting room literature and the final, often fearful, interaction with the dentist.

This clinic occupies 4,000 square feet on the second floor of a forty-year-old building in Beverly Hills. The program required specialized equipment and mechanical services at each dental station; in addition, the reception and waiting area, patient files, X-ray room, and photo lab were to be located within a few feet of the treatment areas.

The existing building was reinforced and adapted for new use with a new elevator, roof structure, plumbing, and electrical system. Over the decades the building had acquired many layers; these had to be removed to determine how the new materials would be applied. The existing structure was treated as a shell, with the new building placed inside it. The relative thinness of the new construction becomes apparent where it attaches to the existing brick-and-concrete structure. Layering the new office within the old container created recesses for natural and artificial indirect lighting and provided ample space.

The scheme consists of five dental stations in one room, separated from one another by steel partitions. Contrary to a simple "free plan" scheme, here the ceiling and walls incorporate floating forms, recessed planes, acute reveals, and unexpected fissures, and splashes of sunlight interrupt fields of diffused light. Each station is marked by a shieldlike prefabricated tower of plywood

and steel that houses almost all of the equipment needed: X-ray machine, operating equipment, plumbing, electrical lines, light table, phone, headphone, and anesthesia delivery system. The operating rooms are designed from the patient's perspective; for instance, the patient's arm-reach radius dictates the room's dimensions.

Seeing the dentist is an act of willing submission, both physical and mental. One assumes a completely defenseless position: prone, on one's back, arms at sides, mouth open. Hovering over the patient are literal strangers, surgical instruments, bright lights—and all the while the patient maintains some state of consciousness typically altered by drugs. One prepares oneself for this submission in the waiting room. Here, this room is a calm, light, nonrectilinear space with an abundance of shadow.

While the scale is relatively intimate, a sense of openness is achieved via a glazed exterior wall and easy access to the corridor that links the five dental stations. The scale also provides a sense of comfort by limiting the dentist's movements, which from the patient's perspective can seem erratic: in more conventional offices the dentist and hygienists frequently disappear from view, moving to and fro for instruments and better positioning. Here the semiopen plan also allows for better circulation.

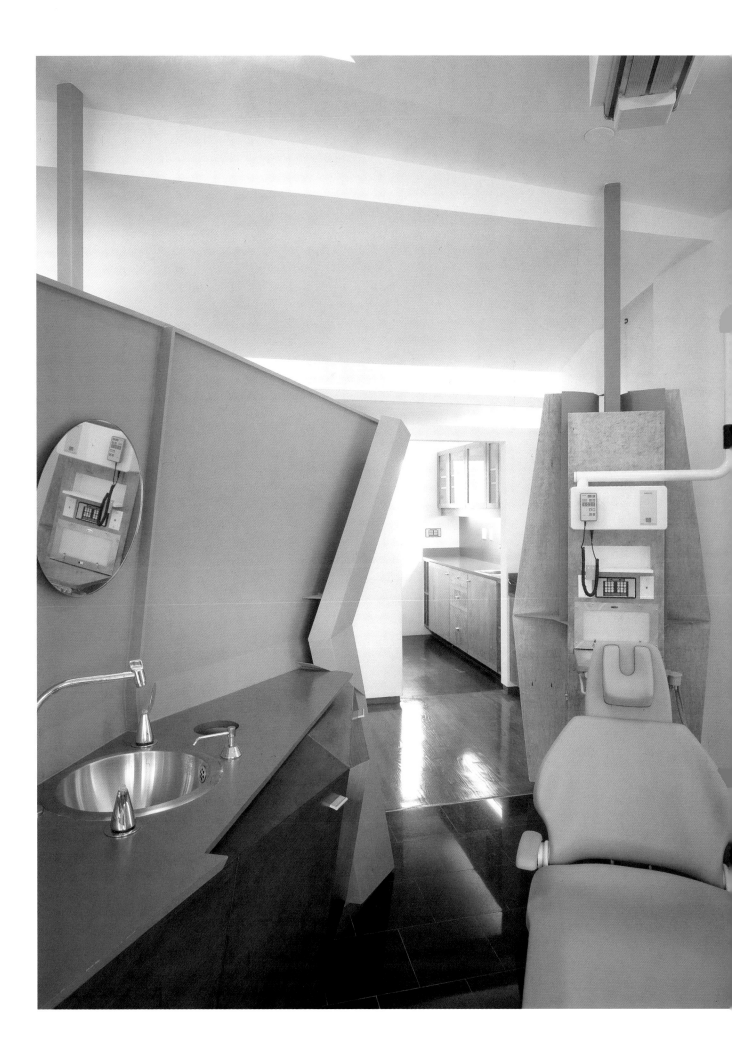

Golzari

[Guest House]

Architecture stems from our desire to find systems of order that allow us to become familiar with our environments and the world around us. These systems, however, are already encoded in the structural, proportional, functional, and organizational principles of architecture; we produce them based on prior knowledge and experience. The systems are fabrications that generate the context of our buildings and the relationships they are based on.

The Golzari Guest House was a rejection of this approach to architecture. The project did not look to the outside for its order, but within. We reasoned that one could discover the origin of an ordering system by looking at the elements that make up the system itself, not at the surrounding information that we divide up and categorize. This approach was, in a sense, a response to the site context and conditions. It was driven by a new way of looking at the site not as a static form to be worked on but as a collection of elements in process, like living organisms, each developing at its own rate.

Here the boundaries between inside and outside were blurred to create a place that is harmonious with both. There is no spatial hierarchy and no distinct sides. The house challenges the typical idea of interior rooms defined by solid partitions, separated into daytime and nighttime spaces, designed for a specific event or use. The goal was to create a space for multiple functions, subject to the will of the user. Overlapping panels allow light to filter into the house and mark the passage of time; as day turns to night, light and shadow pass over the occupants.

The individual pieces that make up the house were designed and shaped much like the templates for the Ecru forms (see p.94); but here, the building becomes the template. No process interrupted the design and build stages, no templates were handed over to a carpenter.

The site is a small, triangular-shaped, hillside lot between two roads. The house was pushed to the front of the lot to create a secure and comfortable backyard. The house steps down the slope, responding to rather than altering the hillside, connecting with the street to eliminate the buffer that is the typical Southern California front yard.

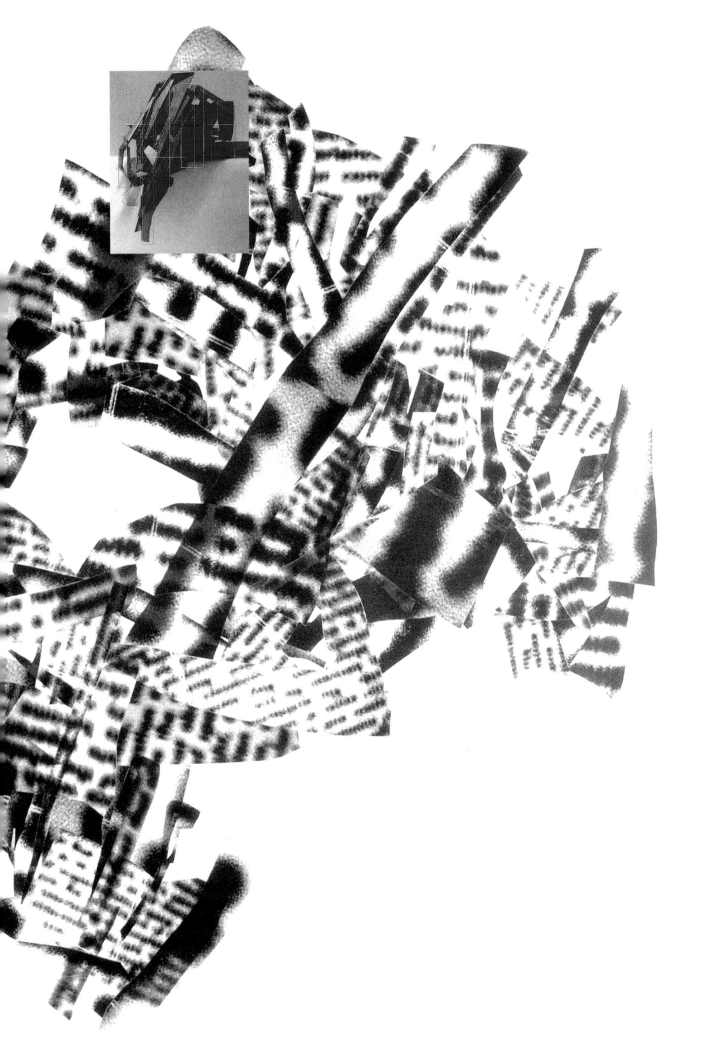

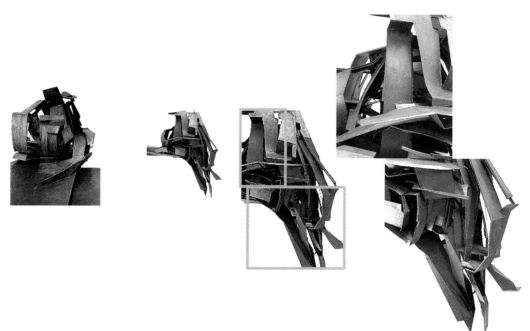

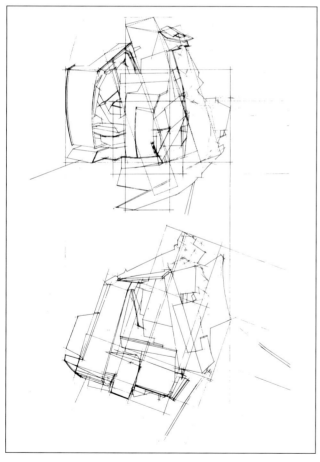

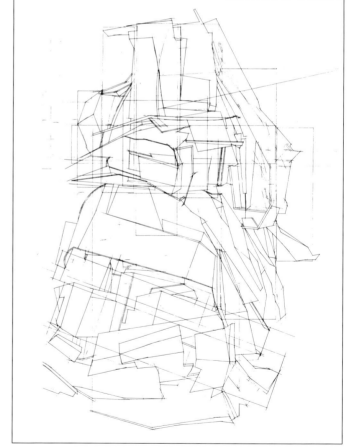

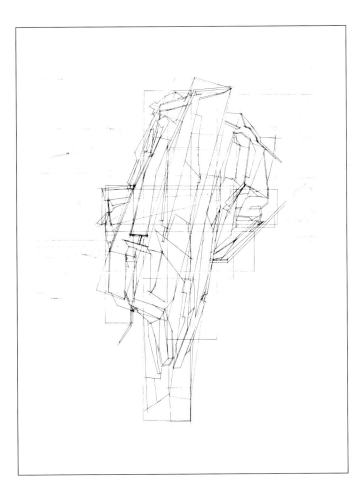

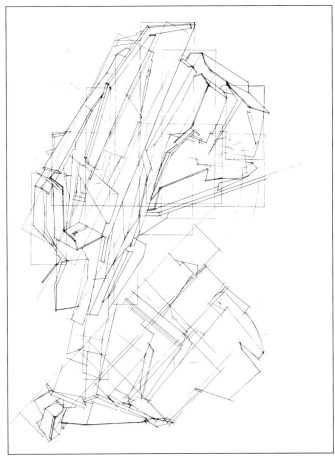

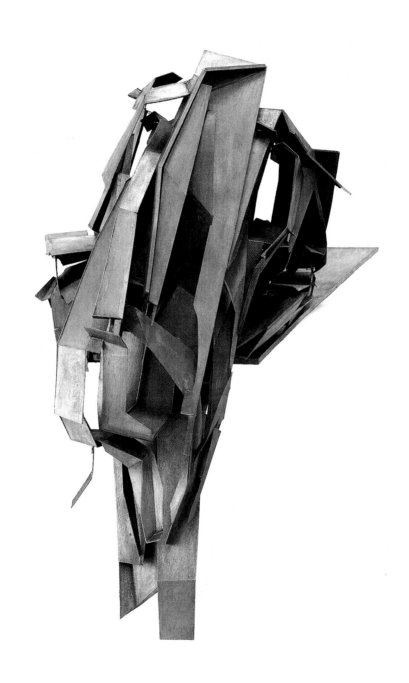

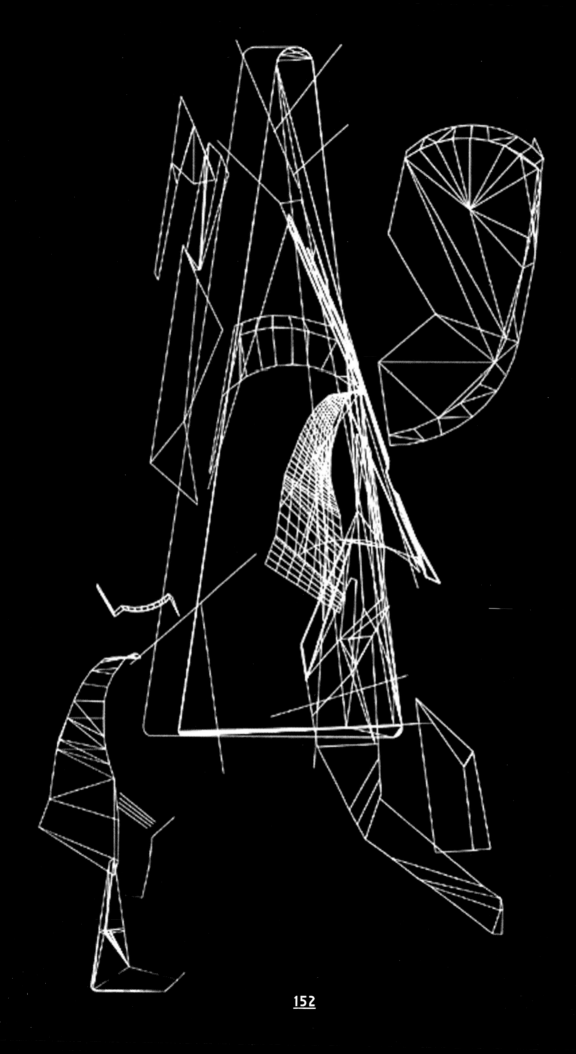

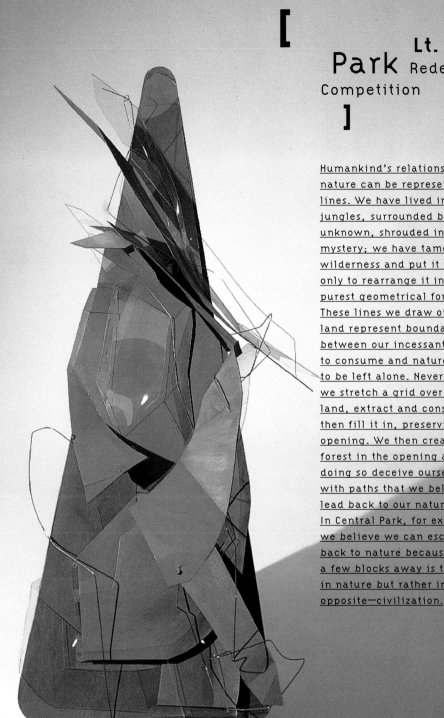

[
Park
Lt. Petrosino
Redevelopment
Competition
]

Humankind's relationship to nature can be represented in lines. We have lived in the jungles, surrounded by the unknown, shrouded in mystery; we have tamed the wilderness and put it to work, only to rearrange it in the purest geometrical forms. These lines we draw on the land represent boundaries between our incessant desire to consume and nature's will to be left alone. Nevertheless, we stretch a grid over the land, extract and consume it, then fill it in, preserving an opening. We then create a forest in the opening and in doing so deceive ourselves with paths that we believe lead back to our natural side. In Central Park, for example, we believe we can escape back to nature because to be a few blocks away is to be not in nature but rather in its opposite—civilization.

Petrosino Park is an attempt to draw new lines that connect rather than separate us from nature. The project offers a new definition of an urban park that does not reject the city environment but rather uses the natural environment as a model for the design of an urban place. The park is buried in a dense urban district of New York and is shaped like an elongated triangle with a 30-foot base and 80-foot sides. Bounded by an iron fence, raised on a concrete piloti, surrounded by a sidewalk, parked cars, busy streets, and an intersection, it is a site generated by urban planning rules.

In our proposal there are no defined pathways in the park: visitors invent paths as they move about and over steel-frame forms coated in seamless rubber roofing material. There are also no benches; visitors notice inviting spots suggested by shade, structures of different heights, and flat areas. Rather than dictating where to sit or walk with functional, predefined elements, the park allows each visitor to experience the place differently. Petrosino Park allows us to see the city not as a collection of static pieces with a prescribed function, but as a place where use is determined by the user. Here, Mother Nature has been removed, and only ideas remain.

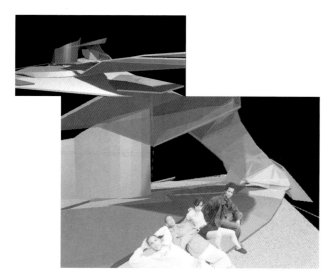

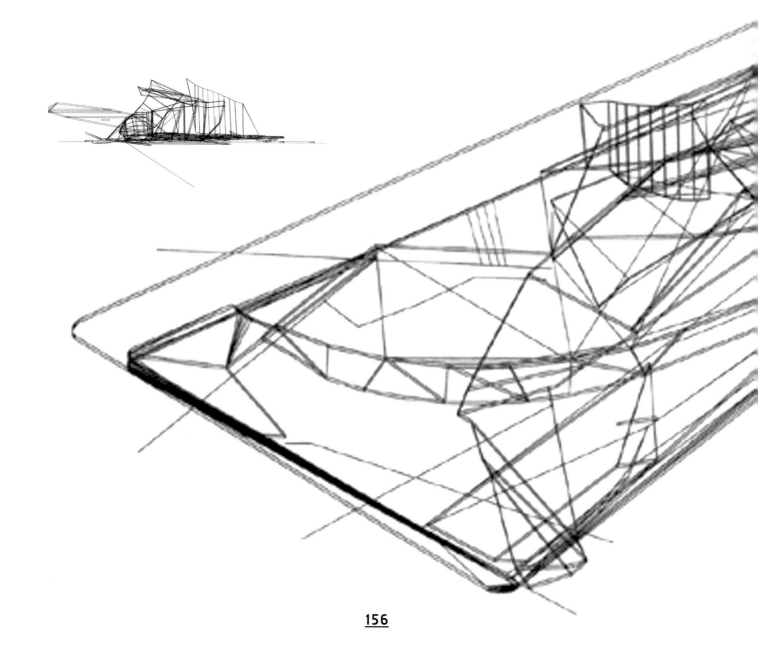

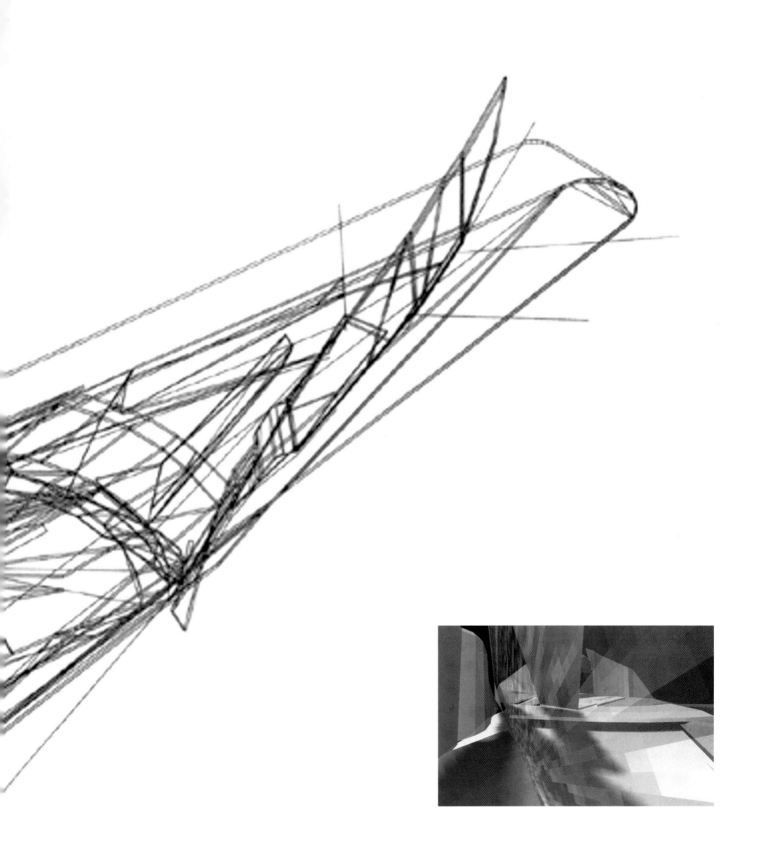

Betsky, Aaron. Violated Perfec-
tion: Architecture and the
Fragmentation of the Modern
(New York: Rizzoli International
Publications, 1990).

Betsky, Aaron, et al. Experimental
Architecture in Los Angeles
(New York: Rizzoli International
Publications, 1991).

Blackwell, Louis. International
Interiors (London: Thames &
Hudson, 1990).

Centre de la Création
Contemporaine. L'Objet de
L'Architecture: Un État de la
Collection du FRAC Centre
(Tours: Centre de la Création
Contemporaine, 1986).

Danto, Arthur C. 397 Chairs
(New York: Harry N. Abrams,
1988).

Frassinelli, Gianpiero. Italian Set
Design, Palcoscenico e Spazio
Scenico (Amsterdam: House of the
Four Winds, 1983).

Jencks, Charles. Heteropolis
(New York: Academy Editions,
Ernst + Sohn, 1993)

Steele, James. Los Angeles
Architecture: The Contemporary
Condition (London: Phaidon Press
Ltd., 1993).

Toy, Maggie, ed. World Cities/Los
Angeles (London: Academy
Editions, 1994).

1995
Russell, Beverly. "Forty Under Forty," Interiors, September 1995.

1994
Betsky, Aaron. "Esperimenti di Architettura," Area (Italy), September 1994.

———. "Weg, Muur, Skelet De Verbeelding van de Californische Droom," de Architect (The Netherlands), September 1994.

Giovannini, Joseph. "L.A. Architects: They Did It Their Way," Los Angeles Times, May 15, 1994.

1992
Newman, Morris. "The Curvature of Space," Progressive Architecture, September 1992.

1991
Fuhrmann, Donna. "Trans Cities Wind: Los Angeles (Restaurant: Angeli Mare/Boutique: Ecru)," WIND (World Interior Design) (Japan), Autumn 1991.

" Meivsahna House," GA: Global Architecture Houses, 1991.

" SCI-Arc," Kenchiku Bunka (Japan), April 1991.

1990
Bates, Colleen Dunn. "Stressed for Success," L.A. Weekly, February 1990.

Betsky, Aaron. "Metallica: The Beauty and Nightmare of Technology," L.A. Weekly, April 1990.

Freiman, Ziva. "Out on Limb," Progressive Architecture, April 1990.

Halliburton, L.N. "Great Spaces: The Architects of Dining in LA," Los Angeles Times, June 1990.

Iovine, Julie I. "Kitchens That Cook: Hot News, Cool Choices," Metropolitan Home, May 1990.

Matsumoto, Kiyo. "Trans Cities Wind: Los Angeles (Boutique: Ecru)," WIND (World Interior Design), Summer 1990.

Michel, Florence. "Le Corps en Morceaux d'Architecture," Architecture Intérieure (France), October/November 1990.

Moore, Rowan. "Complexity and Contradiction," Blueprint, May 1990.

Webb, Michael. "Spirit of the Ocean," Restaurant/Hotel Design International, May 1990.

"The Vigorous Movement Toward the 21st Century of American Designers," Portfolio (Japan), February/March 1990.

1989
"Architectural Designs On a User Friendly Scale," Los Angeles Times, January 10, 1989.

Betsky, Aaron. "Steel and Stucco Dreams: At The L.A. Lab," Metropolitan Home, August 1989.

Chesterfield, Mary. "Inside Outer Spaces," L. A. Style, March 1989.

De Giorgi, Manolo, and Michele Saee. "Tre Ristoranti di Cucina Straniera," Domus, January 1989.

Freiman, Ziva. "Conspicuously for Consumption," Progressive Architecture, June 1989.

Gray, Virginia. "Modern Context" Los Angeles Times Magazine, February 19, 1989.

Kaplan, Sam Hall, and Mary Rourke. "Stylish Display," Los Angeles Times Magazine, March 26, 1989.

Owen, William. "Fractured Facade" and "California Beaming," Designers' Journal (Great Britain), April 1989.

Saee, Michele. "Gehry On Main Street," The Architect's Journal (Great Britain), January 1989.

" Trans Cities Wind: Los Angeles (Trattoria Angeli)," WIND (World Interior Design), Spring 1989.

" Trattoria Angeli and Design Express Furniture Showroom," WIND (World Space Design), 1989.

1988
Freiman, Jane. "Home Style Italian Arrives in L.A.," Cook's, September 1988.

Knox, Barbara J. "Goldin's Rule," Lighting Dimensions, April 1988.

Leighton, John. "Facadismo: Putting up a Good Front," Angeles, October 1988.

Stabiner, Karen. "Birth of a Restaurant," Los Angeles Times Magazine, February 14, 1988.

Stephens, Suzanne. "Sculptured, In and Out," The New York Times, December 29, 1988.

Viladas, Pilar. "Form Follows Feelings," Progressive Architecture, September 1988.

Webb, Michael. "Sequel To Success," Restaurant/Hotel Design Magazine, April 1988.

1987
" In Progress," Progressive Architecture, October 1987.

1986
Rand, George. "Design and the Experience of Dining," Architecture, April 1986.

1985
Brenner, Douglas. "Thought for Food," Architectural Record, September 1985.

Projects in **bold** are included in this volume. All projects are in California unless otherwise noted.

1996

Lt. Petrosino Park
Redevelopment Competition
New York
Client: Lower Manhattan
Cultural Council, Storefront
for Art & Architecture
Principal: Building/Michele Saee

House IS
Saee House
Los Angeles
Client: Arezou, Sayeh, and
Alisina Saee
Principal: Building/Michele Saee

Golzari Guest House
Westlake
Client: Maryam and Madjid Golzari
Principal: Building/Michele Saee

Burger/Schmidt House
Venice
Client: Shelly Burger and
Lohtar Schmidt
Principal: Building/Michele Saee

Dance Studio
Los Angeles
Client: Dance, Inc.
Principal: Building/Michele Saee

Saee Studio
Los Angeles
Client: Michele Saee

1995

Golzari Residence Instances
Westlake
Client: Maryam and Madjid Golzari
(in progress)

1994

"proprioception"
Installation
School of Architecture,
Florida A&M University
Tallahassee, Florida
Client: Florida A&M University

"Art Works for Children"
Installation, Los Angeles
Client: City of Los Angeles

Jacks House
Bel Air
Client: Dr. Madjid Golzari

1993

Arc-Angeli Cafe at the
Southern California Institute
of Architecture (Sci-Arc)
Los Angeles
Client: Evan Kleiman

Atwater Tea + Coffee House
Atwater Village
Client: Saee Family

1992

Angeli Restaurant
in the Rodeo Collection
Beverly Hills
Client: Maison Angeli, Inc.

Beverly Hills Cosmetic
Dental Clinic
Beverly Hills
Client: Dr. Janet Rofua and
Dr. Farzad Okhovat

1991

Pave Jewelry Store
Brentwood
Client: Donna and Peter Edelson

Angeli Mare
Marina del Rey
Client: Evan Kleiman and
John Strobel

1990

Sun House
Fullerton
Client: Sun Family

Township House
Grosse Ile, Michigan
Client: Burke Family
Partnership
(project)

Meivsahna House
Los Angeles
Client: Kleiman/Saee

Piazzale Roma Competition
Venice Biennale
Venice, Italy
Client: City of Venice

Ecru Marina Clothing Store
Marina del Rey
Client: Elaine Kim and Ken Fasola

Wall Clock
Los Angeles
Client: Elika
(unrealized)

1989

434 Apartments
Los Angeles
Client: Building and Company

1988

Chapman-Jones House
Brentwood
Client: Amy Jones and
Michael Chapman

Ecru Clothing Store, Phase II
Los Angeles
Client: Elaine Kim and Ken Fasola

Design Express Warehouse
and Furniture Store
Los Angeles
Client: Hyon and Jim Noh

Osteria Nonni Restaurant
Atwater
Client: Saee Family

1987

Ecru Melrose, Phase I
Los Angeles
Client: Elaine Kim and Ken Fasola

Capitaine Restaurant
Sherman Oaks
Client: Kamadoya U.S.A., Inc.

1986

Trattoria Angeli
Los Angeles
Client: Evan Kleiman and
John Strobel

Borgen Street House
Los Angeles
Client: Arnulf Dickmann
(project)

Field/Piercy House-Studio
Santa Monica
Client: Ann Field and Clive Piercy

"Stage and Set Design"
Los Angeles
Client: Otis Art Institute of
Parsons School of Design

1985

Trattoria Primizia
Santa Cruz
Client: Catherine Algermissen

Sprecher House
Pacific Palisades
Client: Ann Sprecher

Steel I-Beam Chair
Alberti's Shadow Coffee Table